GW01035595

PREVENTING WAR AND DIS/
A GROWING GLOBAL CHALI

Preventing War and Disaster

A Growing Global Challenge

Kofi A. Annan, Secretary-General
of the United Nations

1999 Annual Report
on the work of the Organization

Published by the United Nations
Department of Public Information
New York 10017

United Nations Sales No. E.99.I.29
ISBN 92-1-100826-3
Litho in United Nations, New York

Contents

Introduction

Facing the humanitarian challenge

1. Confronting the horrors of war and natural disasters, the United Nations has long argued that prevention is better than cure; that we must address the root causes, not merely their symptoms. Our aspiration has yet to be matched by effective action, however. As a consequence, the international community today confronts unprecedented humanitarian challenges.

2. The year 1998 was the worst on record for weather-related natural disasters. Floods and storms killed tens of thousands of people worldwide and displaced millions more. When the victims of earthquakes are included, some 50,000 lives were lost last year to natural disasters. Meanwhile, what had seemed a gradual but hopeful trend towards a world with fewer and less deadly wars may have halted. Armed conflicts broke out or erupted anew in Angola, Guinea-Bissau, Kashmir and Kosovo, and between Eritrea and Ethiopia. Other long-established wars, notably that in the Democratic Republic of the Congo, ground on largely unreported by the global media. Moreover, the impact of wars on civilians has worsened because internal wars, now the most frequent type of armed conflict, typically take a heavier toll on civilians than inter-State wars, and because combatants increasingly have made targeting civilians a strategic objective. This brutal disregard for humanitarian norms—and for the Geneva Conventions on the rules of war, whose fiftieth anniversary we recently commemorated—also extends to treatment of humanitarian workers, who are all too frequently denied access to victims in conflict zones or are themselves attacked.

3.   Confronted with renewed armed conflict and the rapidly escalating human and financial costs of natural disasters, our task is twofold. On the one hand, we must strengthen our capacity to bring relief to victims; chapter III of the present report, together with my report to the Security Council on the protection of civilians in armed conflict, addresses in detail how our humanitarian response strategies can be improved. On the other hand, we must devise more effective strategies to prevent emergencies from arising in the first place. The case for better and more cost-effective prevention strategies is my central theme in this introduction.

The scope of the challenge

4.   The world has experienced three times as many great natural disasters in the 1990s as in the 1960s, while emergency aid funds have declined by 40 per cent in the past five years alone, according to the International Federation of Red Cross and Red Crescent Societies.

5.   In the Caribbean, hurricanes Georges and Mitch killed more than 13,000 people in 1998, Mitch being the deadliest Atlantic storm in 200 years. A much less publicized June cyclone in India caused damage comparable to Mitch and an estimated 10,000 deaths.

6.   Major floods hit Bangladesh, India, Nepal and much of East Asia, with thousands killed. Two thirds of Bangladesh was inundated for months, making millions homeless. More than 3,000 died in China's catastrophic Yangtze flood, millions were displaced, and the financial cost is estimated to have been an astonishing $30 billion. Fires ravaged tens of thousands of square kilometres of for-

est in Brazil, Indonesia and Siberia, with devastating consequences for human health and local economies. In Afghanistan, earthquakes killed more than 9,000 people. In August 1999, Turkey suffered one of the most devastating earthquakes in recent history.

7.   In terms of violent conflicts, the most worrying development in 1998 was a significant increase in the number of wars. This is particularly troubling because the incidence and severity of global warfare had been declining since 1992—by a third or more, according to some researchers.

8.   The humanitarian challenge is heightened by the fact that the international community does not respond in a consistent way to humanitarian emergencies. Media attention is part of the problem. The crisis in Kosovo, for example, received saturation coverage. The more protracted and deadly war between Eritrea and Ethiopia, and the resumption of Angola's savage civil war, received very little. Other wars went almost entirely unreported. Partly for that reason, responses to appeals for humanitarian and security assistance have been similarly skewed. Such assistance should not be allocated on the basis of media coverage, politics or geography. Its sole criterion should be human need.

9.   I am particularly alarmed by the international community's poor response to the needs of victims of war and natural disasters in Africa. Where needs are pressing, if we are not true to our most basic principles of multilateralism and humanitarian ethics, we will be accused of inconsistency at best, hypocrisy at worst.

Understanding causes: the first step to successful prevention

10.   Devising preventive strategies that work requires that we first have a clear understanding of under-

lying causes. With respect to disasters the answers are relatively straightforward; war is a more complicated story.

11. Human communities will always face natural hazards—floods, droughts, storms or earthquakes; but today's disasters are sometimes man-made, and human action—or inaction—exacerbates virtually all of them. The term "natural disaster" has become an increasingly anachronistic misnomer. In reality, human behaviour transforms natural hazards into what should really be called unnatural disasters.

12. Poverty and population pressures increase the costs of natural hazards because more and more people have been forced to live in harm's way—on flood plains, earthquake-prone zones and unstable hillsides. It is no accident that more than 90 per cent of all disaster victims worldwide live in developing countries.

13. Unsustainable development practices also contribute to the ever greater impact of natural hazards. Massive logging operations reduce the soil's capacity to absorb heavy rainfall, making erosion and flooding more likely. The destruction of wetlands reduces the ability of the land to soak up run-off, which in turn increases the risk of flooding. In 1998, an estimated 25 million people were driven off their lands into overcrowded and often disaster-prone cities by these and related forms of environmental malpractice.

14. While the earth has always experienced natural cycles of warming and cooling, the 14 hottest years since measurements first began in the 1860s have occurred in the past two decades, and 1998 was the hottest year on record. Although still contested in some quarters, the evidence is steadily accumulating that the current wave of warming and the extreme climatic events associated with it are the product of increased carbon emissions, a large fraction of which is generated by human activity.

15.   The causes of war are inherently more difficult to explain than those of natural events. Social behaviour is not subject to physical laws in the same way as cyclones or earthquakes; people make their own history, often violently and sometimes inexplicably. Causality is therefore complex and multidimensional, and it differs, often fundamentally, from war to war.

16.   We can, however, identify some conditions that increase the probability of war. In recent years poor countries have been far more likely to become embroiled in armed conflicts than rich ones. Yet poverty per se appears not to be the decisive factor; most poor countries live in peace most of the time.

17.   A study recently completed by the United Nations University shows that countries that are afflicted by war typically also suffer from inequality among domestic social groups. It is this, rather than poverty, that seems to be the critical factor. The inequality may be based on ethnicity, religion, national identity or economic class, but it tends to be reflected in unequal access to political power that too often forecloses paths to peaceful change.

18.   Economic decline is also strongly associated with violent conflict, not least because the politics of a shrinking economy are inherently more conflictual than those of economic growth. In some instances the impact of radical market-oriented economic reforms and structural adjustment programmes imposed without compensating social policies can undermine political stability. More generally, weak Governments—and, of course, so-called failed States—have little capacity to stop the eruption and spread of violence that better organized and more legitimate Governments could have prevented or contained.

19.   The shift from war-proneness to war itself can be triggered by the deliberate mobilization of grievances,

and by ethnic, religious or nationalist myth mongering and the promotion of dehumanizing ideologies, all of them too often propagated by hate media. The widespread rise of what is sometimes called identity politics, coupled with the fact that fewer than 20 per cent of all States are ethnically homogeneous, means that political demagogues have little difficulty finding targets of opportunity and mobilizing support for chauvinist causes. The upsurge of "ethnic cleansing" in the 1990s provides stark evidence of the appalling human costs that this vicious exploitation of identity politics can generate.

20.   In other cases, armed conflict has less to do with ethnic, national or other enmities than the struggle to control economic resources. The pursuit of diamonds, drugs, timber concessions and other valuable commodities drives a number of today's internal wars. In some countries, the capacity of the State to extract resources from society and to allocate patronage to cronies or political allies is the prize to be fought over. In others, rebel groups and their backers command most of the resources—and the patronage that goes with them.

Strategies for prevention

21.   Taking prevention more seriously will help to ensure that there are fewer wars and less consequential disasters to cope with in the first place. There is a clear financial incentive for doing so. In the 1960s, natural disasters caused some $52 billion in damage; in the 1990s, the cost has already reached $479 billion. The costs of armed conflict are equally sobering. The Carnegie Commission on Preventing Deadly Conflict estimates that the cost to the international community of the seven major wars in the 1990s, not including Kosovo, was $199 billion. This was in

addition to the costs to the countries actually at war. The Carnegie researchers argued that most of these costs could have been saved if greater attention had been paid to prevention.

22.   More effective prevention strategies would not only save tens of billions of dollars, but hundreds of thousands of lives as well. Funds currently spent on intervention and relief could be devoted to enhancing equitable and sustainable development instead, which would further reduce the risks of war and disaster.

23.   Building a culture of prevention is not easy, however. While the costs of prevention have to be paid in the present, its benefits lie in the distant future. Moreover, the benefits are not tangible; they are the wars and disasters that do not happen. So we should not be surprised that preventive policies receive support that is more often rhetorical than substantive.

24.   This is not all. History tells us that single-cause explanations of either war or natural disaster are invariably too simplistic. This means that no simple, all-embracing, solutions are possible either. To address complex causes we need complex, interdisciplinary solutions. The fundamental point is that implementing prevention strategies—for wars or disasters—requires cooperation across a broad range of different agencies and departments.

25.   Unfortunately, international and national bureaucracies have yet to remove the institutional barriers to building the cross-sector cooperation that is a prerequisite of successful prevention. For example, in national Governments as well as international agencies, departments that are responsible for security policy tend to have little knowledge of development and governance policies, while those responsible for the latter rarely think of them in security terms. Overcoming the barriers posed by organizational di-

vision requires dedicated leadership and a strong commitment to creating "horizontal" interdisciplinary policy networks that include our partners in international civil society.

Disaster prevention

26.   Disaster prevention seeks to reduce the vulnerability of societies to the effects of disasters and also to address their man-made causes. Early warning is especially important for short-term prevention. Advance warning of famine facilitates relief operations; advance warning of storms and floods allows people to move out of harm's way in time. Improvements in wide-area satellite surveillance technologies are revolutionizing the collection of early warning data relevant to disaster prevention.

27.   United Nations agencies are playing an increasingly important early warning role. For example, the Food and Agriculture Organization of the United Nations provides vital warning on impending famines, while the World Meteorological Organization provides support for tropical cyclone forecasting and drought monitoring. The Internet is facilitating the real-time dissemination of satellite-derived and other warning data.

28.   Greater efforts are also being put into contingency planning and other preparedness measures for disaster-prone countries, while major improvements in risk-assessment and loss-estimation methodologies have been identified through the International Decade for Natural Disaster Reduction. As a result of these and other innovations, national Governments are increasingly aware of the dangers and costs imposed by inappropriate land use and environmental practices.

29.   There is also growing consensus on what must be done. Stricter limits should be placed on residential and commercial development in hazardous areas—vulnerable flood plains, hillsides prone to slippage, or fault zones. Construction codes should ensure more resilient buildings as well as infrastructure that can maintain essential services when disaster does strike. Sounder environmental practices are also necessary, particularly with respect to deforestation of hillsides and the protection of wetlands. Moreover, because poverty rather than choice drives people to live in disaster-prone areas, disaster prevention strategies, to be truly effective, should be integrated into overall development policies.

30.   The experience of the International Decade for Natural Disaster Reduction shows that a key to successful longer-term prevention strategies is broad-based cross-sectoral and interdisciplinary cooperation. The campaign to reduce carbon emissions and slow global warming illustrates what can be achieved with such cooperation. Working closely together and guided by the expert consensus that evolved in the Intergovernmental Panel on Climate Change, the scientific community and national and local Governments, together with non-governmental organizations, have been highly successful in alerting the international community to the threats posed by global warming.

31.   Here too, we have ample evidence for the benefits of prevention. As severe as last year's floods in China were, the death toll would have been far higher without the extensive disaster prevention efforts China has undertaken over the years. Floods on a similar scale in 1931 and 1954 claimed more than 140,000 and 33,000 lives respectively—in contrast to 3,000 in 1998. Likewise, hurricane Mitch claimed between 150 and 200 lives in one Honduran village, but none in an equally exposed village nearby,

where a disaster reduction pilot programme had been in operation for some time.

32. We should not underestimate the challenges, however. In some areas, we still lack a broad scientific consensus on core issues and many questions remain unanswered. The problem often lies not so much in achieving consensus among scientists as in persuading Governments to resist pressures from vested interests opposed to change.

33. Resources are a pervasive concern. Some Governments, particularly in the poorest developing countries, simply lack the funds for major risk-reduction and disaster-prevention programmes. International assistance is critical here; and, because preparedness and prevention programmes can radically reduce the future need for humanitarian aid and reconstruction costs, such assistance is highly cost-effective.

34. Education is essential, and not just in schools. Many national Governments and local communities have long pursued appropriate and successful indigenous risk-reduction and mitigation strategies. Finding ways to share that knowledge, and to couple it with the expertise of the scientific community and the practical experience of non-governmental organizations, should be encouraged.

35. For all of these reasons it is essential that the pioneering work carried out during the International Decade for Natural Disaster Reduction be continued. In July 1999, the programme forum on the Decade set out a strategy for the new millennium, "A safer world in the twenty-first century: risk and disaster reduction". It has my full support.

Preventing war

36. For the United Nations, there is no higher goal, no deeper commitment and no greater ambition than pre-

venting armed conflict. The main short- and medium-term strategies for preventing non-violent conflicts from escalating into war, and preventing earlier wars from erupting again, are preventive diplomacy, preventive deployment and preventive disarmament. "Post-conflict peace-building" is a broad policy approach that embraces all of these as well as other initiatives. Longer-term prevention strategies address the root causes of armed conflict.

37.   Whether it takes the form of mediation, conciliation or negotiation, preventive diplomacy is normally non-coercive, low-key and confidential in its approach. Its quiet achievements are mostly unheralded; indeed it suffers from the irony that when it does succeed, nothing happens. Sometimes, the need for confidentiality means that success stories can never be told. As former Secretary-General U Thant once remarked, "the perfect good offices operation is one which is not heard of until it is successfully concluded or even never heard of at all". It is not surprising, therefore, that preventive diplomacy is so often unappreciated by the public at large.

38.   In some trouble spots, the mere presence of a skilled and trusted Special Representative of the Secretary-General can prevent the escalation of tensions; in others more proactive engagement may be needed. In September and October 1998, interventions by my Special Envoy for Afghanistan prevented escalating tensions between Iran and Afghanistan from erupting into war. That vital mission received little publicity, yet its cost was minimal and it succeeded in averting what could have been a massive loss of life.

39.   Preventive diplomacy is not restricted to officials. Private individuals as well as national and international civil society organizations have played an increasingly active role in conflict prevention, management and

resolution. So-called "citizen diplomacy" sometimes paves the way for subsequent official agreements. For example, former United States President Jimmy Carter's visit to Pyongyang in June 1994 helped to resolve a crisis over the nuclear weapons programme of the Democratic People's Republic of Korea and set in motion a process that led directly to an agreement in October that year between that country and the United States of America. In the Middle East peace process, it was a small Norwegian research institute that played the critical initial role in paving the way for the 1993 Oslo Agreement.

40.   In addressing volatile situations that could lead to violent confrontation, Governments are increasingly working in partnership with civil society organizations to defuse tensions and seek creative resolutions to what are often deep-seated problems. In Fiji, for example, collaboration between non-governmental organizations and government officials, aided by quiet diplomacy on the part of regional States, resulted in the promulgation of a new constitution and forestalled what many observers believed was a real possibility of violent conflict.

41.   Early warning is also an essential component of preventive strategy and we have steadily improved our capacity to provide it, often in partnership with regional organizations, such as the Organization of African Unity. The failures of the international community to intervene effectively in Rwanda and elsewhere were not due to a lack of warning, however. In the case of Rwanda, what was missing was the political willingness to use force in response to genocide. The key factors here were the reluctance of Member States to place their forces in harm's way in a conflict where no perceived vital interests were at stake, a concern over cost, and doubts—in the wake of Somalia—that intervention could succeed.

42.   Complementing preventive diplomacy are preventive deployment and preventive disarmament. Like peacekeeping, preventive deployment is intended to provide a "thin blue line" to help contain conflicts by building confidence in areas of tension or between highly polarized communities. To date, the only specific instance of the former has been the United Nations mission to the former Yugoslav Republic of Macedonia. Such deployments have been considered in other conflicts and remain an underutilized but potentially valuable preventive option.

43.   Preventive disarmament seeks to reduce the number of small arms and light weapons in conflict-prone regions. In El Salvador, Mozambique and elsewhere this has entailed demobilizing combat forces as well as collecting and destroying their weapons as part of the implementation of an overall peace agreement. Destroying yesterday's weapons prevents their being used in tomorrow's wars.

44.   Preventive disarmament efforts are also increasingly directed towards slowing small arms and light weapons trafficking, the only weapons used in most of today's armed conflicts. These weapons do not cause wars, but they can dramatically increase both their lethality and their duration. I firmly support the various initiatives to curtail this lethal trade that are currently being pursued within the United Nations, at the regional level and by non-governmental organization coalitions.

45.   What has come to be known as post-conflict peace-building is a major and relatively recent innovation in preventive strategy. During the 1990s, the United Nations developed a more holistic approach to implementing the comprehensive peace agreements it negotiated. From Namibia to Guatemala, post-conflict peace-building has involved inter-agency teams working alongside non-governmental organizations and local citizens' groups to

help provide emergency relief, demobilize combatants, clear mines, run elections, build impartial police forces and set in motion longer-term development efforts. The premise of this broad strategy is that human security, good governance, equitable development and respect for human rights are interdependent and mutually reinforcing.

46.   Post-conflict peace-building is important not least because there are far more peace agreements to be implemented today than there were in the past. In fact, three times as many agreements have been signed in the 1990s as in the previous three decades. Some agreements have failed, often amid great publicity, but most have held.

47.   Long-term prevention strategies, in addressing the root causes of conflict, seek to prevent destructive conflicts from arising in the first place. They embrace the same holistic approach to prevention that characterizes post-conflict peace-building. Their approach is reflected in the recent United Nations University study that found that inclusive government is the best guarantor against internal violent conflicts. Inclusiveness requires that all the major groups in a society participate in its major institutions—government, administration, police and the military.

48.   These conclusions are consistent with the so-called "democratic peace thesis", which states that democracies rarely go to war against each other, and that they have low levels of internal violence compared with non-democracies. The former proposition is still the subject of lively debate among academic experts—in part because of the changing meanings of "democracy" across time and geography. The latter proposition is less controversial: in essence, democracy is a non-violent form of internal conflict management.

49.　Long-term prevention embraces far too many strategies to be considered in detail in this essay. Here, I will simply highlight three that are worthy of consideration but have thus far received relatively little attention in the international community.

50.　First, the international community should do more to encourage policies that enhance people-centred security in conflict-prone States. Equitable and sustainable development is a necessary condition for security, but minimum standards of security are also a precondition for development. Pursuing one in isolation from the other makes little sense. Security from organized violence is a priority concern of people everywhere, and ensuring democratic accountability and transparency in the security sector should receive greater support and encouragement from donor States and the international financial institutions. Moreover, since the overwhelming majority of today's armed conflicts take place within, not between, States, it makes good security sense in many cases to shift some of the resources allocated to expensive external defence programmes to relatively low-cost initiatives that enhance human—and hence national—security.

51.　Second, greater effort should be put into ensuring that development policies do not exacerbate the risks of conflict—by increasing inequality between social groups, for example. In this context, the idea of "conflict impact assessments" should be explored further. Such assessments seek, via consultation with a broad range of stakeholders, to ensure that particular development or governance policies at the very least do not undermine security and at best enhance it. The model here is the well-established environmental impact assessment process, which accompanies major development and extractive industry projects in many countries.

52.   Third, the changing realities of the global economy mean new challenges—and new opportunities. During the past decade, development assistance has continued to decline, while private capital flows to the developing world have risen significantly. This has reduced the relative influence of donor States and international institutions in developing countries, while increasing the presence of international corporations. The private sector and security are linked in many ways, most obviously because thriving markets and human security go hand in hand. Global corporations can do more than simply endorse the virtues of the market, however. Their active support for better governance policies can help create environments in which both markets and human security flourish.

53.   The common thread running through almost all conflict prevention policies is the need to pursue what we in the United Nations refer to as good governance. In practice, good governance involves promoting the rule of law, tolerance of minority and opposition groups, transparent political processes, an independent judiciary, an impartial police force, a military that is strictly subject to civilian control, a free press and vibrant civil society institutions, as well as meaningful elections. Above all, good governance means respect for human rights.

54.   We should not delude ourselves, however, into thinking that prevention is a panacea, or that even the best-resourced prevention policies will guarantee peace. Prevention philosophy is predicated on the assumption of good faith, the belief that Governments will seek to place the welfare of the people as a whole over narrow sectional interests. Sadly, we know that this is often not the case. Indeed, many of the requirements of good governance that

are central to prevention stand in stark contradiction to the survival strategies of some of the most conflict-prone Governments.

55.   While providing incentives for progressive change can sometimes help, it is not something that the international community does often or particularly well. The prospect of closer association with the European Union has served as a powerful tool for promoting tolerance and institutional reforms in several East and Central European countries, but few, if any, counterparts exist at the global level.

56.   The fact that even the best prevention strategies can fail means that we can never completely escape the scourge of war. It follows that, for the foreseeable future, the international community must remain prepared to engage politically—and if necessary militarily—to contain, manage and ultimately resolve conflicts that have got out of hand. This will require a better functioning collective security system than exists at the moment. It will require, above all, a greater willingness to intervene to prevent gross violations of human rights.

57.   Demonstrable willingness to act in such circumstances will in turn serve the goal of prevention by enhancing deterrence. Even the most repressive leaders watch to see what they can get away with, how far they can tear the fabric of human conscience before triggering an outraged external response. The more the international community succeeds in altering their destructive calculus, the more lives can be saved.

58.   Collective security in the international system is, of course, the responsibility of the Security Council and responding to crises and emergencies will always be a major focus of its activity. Article 1 of the Charter reminds us that one of the purposes of the United Nations is to take

"effective collective measures for the prevention and removal of threats to the peace". Yet reaction, not prevention, has been the dominant Security Council approach to dealing with conflict over the years. Recently, however, the Council has shown increased interest in tackling prevention issues. This has been evident in the Council's extensive debate on post-conflict peace-building and in its response to my report on the causes of conflict and the promotion of durable peace and sustainable development in Africa, which endorsed a range of conflict prevention measures.

59. I greatly welcome these developments. During the coming year, I intend to continue the dialogue on prevention with the members of the Council, which started with the first Security Council retreat I convened in June 1999.

* * *

60. Today, no one disputes that prevention is better, and cheaper, than reacting to crises after the fact. Yet our political and organizational cultures and practices remain oriented far more towards reaction than prevention. In the words of the ancient proverb, it is difficult to find money for medicine, but easy to find it for a coffin.

61. The transition from a culture of reaction to a culture of prevention will not be easy for the reasons I have outlined, but the difficulty of our task does not make it any less imperative. War and natural disasters remain the major threats to the security of individuals and human communities worldwide. Our solemn duty to future generations is to reduce these threats. We know what needs to be done. What is now needed is the foresight and political will to do it.

1 Achieving peace and security

Introduction

62. During the 1990s, we have witnessed major changes in the patterns of global conflict and in the international community's responses to them. Today, more than 90 per cent of armed conflicts take place within, rather than between, States. With relatively few inter-State wars, traditional rationales for intervention have become decreasingly relevant, while humanitarian and human rights principles have increasingly been invoked to justify the use of force in internal wars, not always with the authorization of the Security Council. Sanctions have been used far more frequently in the 1990s than ever before, but with results that are ambiguous at best.

63. One of the more encouraging developments of the last decade has been an increase in the number of conflicts settled by negotiation. Three times as many peace agreements were signed in the 1990s as in the previous three decades, reflecting a more than 30 per cent decline in the overall number and intensity of armed conflicts around the world from 1992 to 1997. With the sharp upturn in the number of wars in 1998, however, it seems doubtful that the positive trend of the previous five years will be sustained.

64. Comprehensive peace agreements have led to complex implementation processes involving many different agencies. While some traditional peacekeeping operations remain, peacekeepers throughout this decade have been involved in the broader post-conflict peace-building processes associated with the implementation of peace agreements. Post-conflict peace-building involves the return and reintegration of refugees and internally displaced persons, reconciliation, rebuilding judicial systems, strengthening the promotion and protection of human rights, electoral assistance and assistance in rebuilding war-torn political, economic and social infrastructures, as well as more traditional peacekeeping tasks.

65.   In response to the changing international normative climate, the number of legal instruments, particularly relating to humanitarian and human rights law, has increased considerably. Growing public concern about gross human rights violations provided much of the political impetus for the creation of the International Criminal Court; concern about the humanitarian costs of landmines fuelled the successful campaign to ban them.

66.   The past decade has also been a period of tension and difficulty for the United Nations as it has sought to fulfil its collective security mandate. Earlier this year, the Security Council was precluded from intervening in the Kosovo crisis by profound disagreements between Council members over whether such an intervention was legitimate. Differences within the Council reflected the lack of consensus in the wider international community. Defenders of traditional interpretations of international law stressed the inviolability of State sovereignty; others stressed the moral imperative to act forcefully in the face of gross violations of human rights. The moral rights and wrongs of this complex and contentious issue will be the subject of debate for years to come, but what is clear is that enforcement actions without Security Council authorization threaten the very core of the international security system founded on the Charter of the United Nations. Only the Charter provides a universally accepted legal basis for the use of force.

67. Disagreements about sovereignty are not the only impediments to Security Council action in the face of complex humanitarian emergencies. Confronted by gross violations of human rights in Rwanda and elsewhere, the failure to intervene was driven more by the reluctance of Member States to pay the human and other costs of intervention, and by doubts that the use of force would be successful, than by concerns about sovereignty.

Preventive diplomacy and peacemaking

68. Early warning is now universally agreed to be a necessary condition for effective preventive diplomacy. It is not, unfortunately, a sufficient condition, as the tragedy in Kosovo has demonstrated. As the crisis unfolded, I twice addressed the Security Council in the hope that consensus could be achieved for effective preventive action. Regrettably, diplomatic efforts failed, and the destructive logic of developments on the ground prevailed.

69. What lessons should be drawn from this and other recent failures in conflict prevention? First, that if the primacy of the Security Council with respect to the maintenance of international peace and security is rejected, the very foundations of international law as represented by the Charter will be brought into question. No other universally accepted legal basis for constraining wanton acts of violence exists. Second, that conflict prevention, peacekeeping and peacemaking must not become an area of competition between the United Nations and regional organizations. We work together best when we respect each other's prerogatives and sensitivities. Third, that prevention can only succeed with strong political commitment from Member States and if the provision of resources is adequate.

70.   Healing the wounds of a war-torn society is never an easy task. It presents a particularly difficult challenge in Kosovo, which remains embedded in the complicated and contentious political fabric of the Balkans. We recognize the real potential for further disruption of the fragile ethnic equilibrium in a number of the surrounding countries.

71.   While the crisis in Kosovo has dominated global media headlines during the past year, equally or more serious crises in other parts of the world have been largely ignored. If this neglect were restricted to the media it would not be of great consequence, but media inattention reflects the attitude of much of the international community, as has become evident in the decline in support for humanitarian appeals for Africa.

72.   Security developments in Africa continue to cause the gravest concern. In West and Central Africa in particular, the threat that internal conflicts will spread and lead to armed confrontations between sovereign African States is an especially worrying development.

73.   This risk is perhaps best illustrated by the ongoing hostilities in the Democratic Republic of the Congo, in which a large number of African countries have become involved. My Special Envoy, Moustapha Niasse, whom I dispatched to the region in the spring, has been working in support of the diplomatic solution put forward by President Frederick Chiluba, on behalf of the Southern African Development Community. President Chiluba's efforts have the support of the Organization of African Unity (OAU) and the United Nations.

74.   The prospects for peace in the Democratic Republic of the Congo have improved. On 10 July, all the belligerents except the Rassemblement congolais pour la démocratie signed a ceasefire agreement in Lusaka. The Se-

curity Council welcomed the agreement and authorized the deployment of United Nations military and civilian personnel in the region to facilitate the implementation of the ceasefire. After concerted efforts by South Africa, the United Republic of Tanzania, Zambia and others, the disagreement between the Kisangani and Goma factions of the Rassemblement congolais pour la démocratie over who should sign the ceasefire agreement appears to have been resolved. Once the agreement is signed, the United Nations will dispatch a multi-disciplinary technical survey team to the region to assess the security and infrastructure of the areas provisionally identified for future deployments.

75.   The peace process in Burundi has also shown some progress, with the Arusha negotiations, under the leadership of former President Julius Nyerere, having reached a crucial stage.

76.   In Sierra Leone, whose people have been the victims of one of the most brutal conflicts of recent times, the United Nations Observer Mission in Sierra Leone (UNOMSIL) has worked assiduously to help facilitate a negotiated solution. In close cooperation with the Economic Community of West African States (ECOWAS), its Monitoring Group (ECOMOG) and other interested Member States, UNOMSIL actively supported the process of negotiations between the Government and the Revolutionary United Front, which led to the signing on 7 July 1999 of the Lomé Peace Agreement. Following the signing of the Peace Agreement, the Security Council authorized an expansion of UNOMSIL. Recognizing the close relationship between the promotion of human rights and sustainable peace, UNOMSIL, in collaboration with the Office of the United Nations High Commissioner for Human Rights, continues to monitor and report on human rights abuses in Sierra Leone with a view to ending further violations.

77.   The outbreak of war between Eritrea and Ethiopia in May 1998 was also a cause of profound disquiet. I immediately contacted the leaders of both parties, urging restraint and offering assistance in resolving the conflict peacefully. I have maintained contacts with both sides. I also requested Ambassador Mohammed Sahnoun to assist the mediation efforts of OAU as my Special Envoy. Ambassador Sahnoun participated in various meetings organized by OAU and visited the Eritrean and Ethiopian capitals to press for the acceptance of the peace plan, the OAU Framework Agreement.

78.   The conflict between Eritrea and Ethiopia has also had a tragic regional impact, particularly with regard to the conflict in Somalia. The United Nations Political Office for Somalia continues to assist regional efforts at peacemaking in Somalia that are led by the Intergovernmental Authority on Development (IGAD). However, a lack of consensus on the mode of power-sharing among the various factions has precluded settlement of the conflict. The main challenge in the year ahead will be to strengthen international peacemaking efforts and to identify initiatives that can be supported by all the relevant actors.

79.   I have also been closely following the continuing complex humanitarian emergency in the Sudan, where developments again highlight the need to address the root causes of the conflict in order to speed the search for a political solution. In 1998, I visited the area and reiterated my offer of good offices to the parties and the mediators. Following a number of internal and external consultations, we have taken further steps to support and invigorate the IGAD peace initiative on the Sudan. Assisting this process, which sadly has not been sustained, remains our primary objective in the quest to help the parties achieve a just and lasting settlement.

80. The United Nations has been involved for many years in Western Sahara, where recent consultations with the Government of Morocco and the Frente POLISARIO have finally resolved a longstanding impasse over a referendum for self-determination. A new date, 31 July 2000, has been set for the referendum.

81. Africa is not, of course, the only area of security concern for the United Nations. Relations with Iraq took a turn for the worse during the year, despite a brief period of compliance with the Memorandum of Understanding signed by Deputy Prime Minister Tariq Aziz and myself in February 1998. In the face of continuing Iraqi non-compliance, the use of force by two Member States and the division in the Security Council that followed it was predictable. Our principal demands remain unchanged, however: Iraq must fully comply with all relevant Security Council resolutions; the international community must be assured that Iraq no longer has the capacity to develop or use weapons of mass destruction; missing Kuwaiti and third country nationals must be accounted for; and Kuwait's irreplaceable archives must be returned. Meanwhile, the people of Iraq continue to suffer the effects of sanctions, although since December 1996 the oil-for-food programme has helped to alleviate some of the suffering by allowing the delivery of humanitarian goods to the country.

82. The overall situation in the Middle East remains troubling. The international community has expressed its strong support for a comprehensive, just and lasting peace in the Middle East based on relevant Security Council resolutions and the principle of land for peace. The recent resumption of the peace process and indications of a real commitment to achieving a settlement by the key protagonists are grounds for cautious optimism.

83.   In some conflicts, however, hostility is so intense, and distrust so pervasive, that progress becomes
extraordinarily difficult to achieve. This is still the case in
Afghanistan. My Special Envoy for Afghanistan, Lakhdar
Brahimi, visited the region in October 1998 and late in February this year for talks with the authorities of neighbouring countries, as well as with the Taliban and the United
Front. In July of this year, the "six plus two" group held a
meeting in Tashkent following which my Special Envoy
again visited the region. The United Nations Special Mission to Afghanistan succeeded in convening two rounds
of intra-Afghan talks in Ashgabat in February and March
1999. The parties managed to reach an agreement in
principle on the sharing of government institutions. Unfortunately, in mid-spring, the Taliban leadership announced that it would not resume the negotiations started
under United Nations auspices. In July, the Taliban
launched an offensive against the United Front but failed
to gain a decisive advantage. In August, severe fighting
continued with grave humanitarian consequences. Notwithstanding these setbacks, I intend continuing my efforts to persuade both sides to resume consultations and
to draw in interested Member States and the Organization
of the Islamic Conference, where this may be helpful, in
order to explore the prospects for an eventual peace
agreement.

84.   The recent upsurge of fighting along and across
the line of control in Kashmir, especially in the Kargil area,
is a reminder of the fragility of the situation in this region.
The process initiated in Lahore needs to be put back on
track as there are serious grounds for concern, not least because of the dangers of an unintended escalation in a sub-
continent in which nuclear devices have been tested.

85. On 5 May 1999, after intensive diplomatic efforts, Indonesia, Portugal and the United Nations concluded a set of agreements calling for the United Nations to conduct a popular consultation of the East Timorese people on whether they would accept the special autonomy status offered by Indonesia. Rejection of autonomy would lead to East Timor's separation from Indonesia and transition, under United Nations authority, to independent statehood. The United Nations Mission in East Timor (UNAMET) was established by the Security Council on 11 June 1999. A region-wide structure established by the Mission's Electoral Unit completed a successful registration process despite adverse security conditions. UNAMET also organized and conducted a comprehensive voter education campaign, worked with local authorities and East Timorese groups to foster reconciliation, and deployed civilian police and military liaison officers to advise local police and liaise with the Indonesian military on security issues. Following the successful consultation on 30 August, the United Nations will remain in East Timor to assist in implementing the result.

86. The situation in Myanmar is of continuing concern. My Special Envoy, Alvaro de Soto, visited Myanmar in October 1998 to hold consultations with the Myanmar authorities, as well as with other political actors, including Daw Aung San Suu Kyi, General Secretary of the National League for Democracy. Despite our concerted efforts, I am unfortunately unable to report on any genuine, substantive response by the Government of Myanmar to the appeals made to it, in successive resolutions, by the General Assembly.

87. The United Nations Political Office in Bougainville, which was established in August 1998, has played a critical role in facilitating the search for a peaceful resolu-

tion of the crisis in Bougainville, Papua New Guinea. The National Government of Papua New Guinea and the Bougainville parties have asked the Office to supervise the process of disarmament, which will allow implementation of the programme of rehabilitation and reconstruction of the island to begin as soon as possible. The new Government of Papua New Guinea has stressed that the continuation of the peace process is one of its most important objectives.

88.   There have been a number of encouraging signs of improved security relations in Latin America over the past year. The Governments of Ecuador and Peru finally took the steps needed to bring their long-standing border dispute to an end, while Argentina and Chile have also agreed to settle the dispute over their frontier.

Peacekeeping

89.   The past year has been a tumultuous one for United Nations peacekeeping. We are facing major new challenges with the creation of the large-scale, and in many ways unprecedented, operation in Kosovo, with preparations for a complex new mission in the Democratic Republic of the Congo, the expansion of the mission in Sierra Leone, the strong likelihood of a new operation in Eritrea and Ethiopia, the continuing evolution of the situation in Timor, and the recent agreement by the Government of Angola for a continued United Nations presence in that country.

90.   The closure of two major missions, the United Nations Observer Mission in Angola and the United Nations Preventive Deployment Force, and the completion of a follow-on operation, the United Nations Police Support

Group in Croatia, have brought the current number of peacekeeping operations to 16.

91. A sudden deterioration in the security situation led to the evacuation of the United Nations Observation Mission in Sierra Leone in January 1999. The restoration of security in Freetown allowed UNOMSIL to return in March to help in supporting the peace process, which culminated in the signing of the Lomé Peace Agreement on 7 July. The implementation of that Agreement will involve an expanded peacekeeping presence, which we are currently examining with ECOWAS.

92. The volatility and danger of the environments in which the United Nations operates are underlined by the number of casualties suffered by United Nations peacekeepers. From 1 January 1998 to 19 August 1999, 34 United Nations personnel gave their lives in peacekeeping operations. We owe them a debt of gratitude that can never be repaid.

93. Perhaps the most disturbing trend has been the growing contempt for international norms. In addition to the savage attacks on civilians, peacekeepers have also been targeted, or used as pawns to manipulate international public opinion. In this context, I warmly welcome the entry into force of the Convention on the Safety of United Nations and Associated Personnel and I would strongly encourage further ratifications by Member States. In response to these developments, the Department of Peacekeeping Operations is undertaking a systematic review of the problem of violence against peacekeepers. I look forward to informing Member States of its findings as this work progresses.

94. Just as the year was tumultuous for peacekeeping, it was similarly testing for the Department of Peacekeeping Operations. In accordance with the wishes

of the General Assembly, gratis personnel were phased out by the end of February. As a consequence, the Department as a whole has been reduced by almost 20 per cent during the past year. In order to adjust to the new realities, while continuing to perform its mandated functions, the Department underwent a significant restructuring. The creation or expansion of several missions, the closure and liquidation of others, and mandated planning for possible future operations have occurred in this context. Ironically, the logistics and communications area—vital for the deployment of new missions as well as the liquidation of old ones—was hardest hit by the reduction of staff.

95.   This experience shows once again that preparedness requires capacities beyond those needed for current activities. The demand for peacekeeping and other field operations is, by its very nature, difficult to predict and such operations must often be established at short notice. The credibility and effectiveness of any new operation are affected by the promptness with which it is deployed. Delays provide an opportunity for those who oppose the peace process, or the terms of a settlement, to seize the initiative before United Nations personnel arrive. In determining resource requirements for the Organization, including its Headquarters staff, I trust that Member States will bear this in mind.

96.   In spite of the unpredictability of events over the past year, some things remained constant. One was the continued emphasis on multidimensional peacekeeping, which is now the norm for the Organization. Multidimensional peacekeeping operations tackle a number of challenges concurrently: helping to maintain ceasefires and to disarm and demobilize combatants; assisting the parties to build or strengthen vital institutions and processes and respect for human rights, so that all concerned can pursue

their interests through legitimate channels rather than on the battlefield; providing humanitarian assistance to relieve immediate suffering; and laying the groundwork for longer-term economic growth and development on the understanding that no post-conflict system can long endure if it fails to improve the lot of impoverished people. The Organization is continuing to develop the methods to coordinate these diverse activities more effectively.

97.   I have previously reported on ways in which the United Nations programmes, funds and agencies are brought together by my appointed Special Representatives in support of integrated security and development strategies. Additional innovations this year have included our work with the World Bank in the Central African Republic, where the United Nations responsibilities in security, elections and institutional reform have been matched by the Bank's efforts to assist with economic stabilization and to promote longer-term growth. The United Nations Mission in the Central African Republic (MINURCA) played an important supportive role that enabled the peaceful and successful conduct of legislative elections in November/December 1998. MINURCA is to provide support for the presidential elections scheduled for September 1999. Unfortunately, funding for MINURCA is suffering from a worrying lack of enthusiasm among donors, and lack of funding will undoubtedly hamper the efforts of MINURCA to support and observe the elections.

98.   Similarly, in Tajikistan, there was initially a very low donor response to appeals for funds to support demobilization projects, an important aspect of the mandate of the United Nations Mission of Observers in Tajikistan. The resulting delays again point to the drawbacks of funding essential elements of a mandate through voluntary contributions, rather than through assessed contributions as is nor-

mally the case in peacekeeping operations. There has nevertheless been significant progress in advancing the peace process, and we are cautiously optimistic that the Mission's mandate will be fulfilled.

99. The case of Kosovo is the latest in a series of innovations in peacekeeping and post-conflict peace-building that have been pursued in the 1990s in cooperation with regional and subregional organizations. In Kosovo, we are cooperating with the European Union in reconstruction and rehabilitation programmes, and with the Organization for Security and Cooperation in Europe in institution-building. Both of those organizations operate under the authority of my Special Representative. We are also working closely with the international military forces responsible for security in Kosovo to ensure unity of civilian and military efforts.

100. In 1999, the Secretariat, in collaboration with the International Committee of the Red Cross, finalized principles and rules on the observance of international humanitarian law by peacekeepers; these rules have been issued as a Secretary-General's bulletin. I hope that the promulgation of that bulletin will help to clarify the scope of the application of international humanitarian law to United Nations forces and operations and ensure that the required standards are observed.

Post-conflict peace-building

101. Post-conflict peace-building seeks to prevent the resurgence of conflict and to create the conditions necessary for a sustainable peace in war-torn societies. It is a holistic process involving broad-based inter-agency cooperation

across a wide range of issues. It encompasses activities as diverse as traditional peacekeeping and electoral assistance.

102. Achieving the necessary coordination and complementarity between agencies in conflict and fragile post-conflict situations continues to present a major challenge to the United Nations and its partners. Recognizing the scope of this challenge, in 1997 I designated the Department of Political Affairs, in its capacity as convener of the Executive Committee on Peace and Security, as the focal point for post-conflict peace-building.

103. The past year has seen a number of developments in United Nations post-conflict peace-building operations. Activities in the field include forward planning for a future United Nations presence in the Central African Republic when the mandate of MINURCA expires; establishing a new office dedicated to peace-building in Guinea-Bissau; sustaining the major United Nations presence in Guatemala; and consolidating long-standing peace processes in Cambodia and El Salvador and elsewhere.

104. After a year of divisive and destructive conflict in Guinea-Bissau, prospects for a return to normality have improved, albeit gradually. The United Nations Peace-building Support Office is working with the Government and people to coordinate an integrated response to the challenges of peace-building. In Liberia, the United Nations Peace-building Support Office is about to complete its second year of operation. Despite limited financial resources, the Office has supported a number of projects dealing with national reconciliation and rebuilding respect for the rule of law and human rights.

105. The United Nations Verification Mission in Guatemala is mandated by the General Assembly to carry out a

range of post-conflict peace-building activities in addition to verifying the peace agreements, providing good offices and undertaking advisory and public information activities. Since 1997, considerable emphasis has been placed on human rights, particularly indigenous rights; social investment; decentralization of State activities; rural development; fiscal and judicial reforms; and the reform of public security and national defence. In 1998, these initiatives provided the basis for a constitutional reform package, which was approved by Congress but which the people failed to ratify in a national referendum in May 1999. As presidential and legislative elections approach in November 1999, continuing commitment to the peace agenda will be crucial to its sustainability.

106. In neighbouring El Salvador, the United Nations Development Programme (UNDP) is responsible for assisting the Government with peace accord issues that remain unresolved. UNDP works in close coordination with the Department of Political Affairs, which retains responsibility for good offices. One of the greatest challenges facing the newly inaugurated Government is consolidation of the institutions that were created, or reformed, as part of the peace process, particularly those responsible for dealing with the country's public security crisis and the protection and promotion of human rights.

107. Institution-building, particularly of the judicial sector, and the protection and promotion of human rights are the key tasks of the International Civilian Mission in Haiti (MICIVIH). As in previous years, there remains much to be done to strengthen State institutions and civil society organizations. The reduced participation of the Organization of American States in MICIVIH, as from 1 July 1999, will necessarily affect our continued role, although core functions will continue to be performed. Meanwhile, the

United Nations and the international community have pledged to support the holding of legislative and local government elections by the end of 1999—a crucial requirement for Haiti's future progress.

108. During the past year, there have been welcome developments in Cambodia. With the establishment of a new Government and the collapse of the Khmer Rouge movement, the country is finally at peace and able to devote its attention to reconstruction. My Personal Representative in Cambodia and the United Nations agencies in the country remain committed to assisting the Government in its nation-building efforts, including the strengthening of democratic institutions and assistance in the promotion and protection of human rights.

Electoral assistance

109. In the late 1980s and early 1990s, the implementation of comprehensive peace agreements in Angola, Cambodia, El Salvador, Mozambique and Nicaragua required the presence of major United Nations electoral missions to help organize the mandated elections. Often viewed as the final step in a long-term peacemaking process, elections symbolize the re-establishment of national authority in a new multi-party system of government. Experience has demonstrated, however, that the relationship of elections to the long-term process of peace-building is highly complex. As the "age of democratization" has entered into a new phase, the Organization has shifted its electoral assistance strategy to encompass a broader understanding of post-conflict peace-building. Elections that have in the past served predominantly as an exit strategy out of conflict situations are now seen as providing an opportunity for institution-building and the introduction of programmes for good governance.

110. Elections are a necessary, but not sufficient, condition for creating viable democracies. That requires the establishment or strengthening of democratic infrastructures such as electoral commissions, electoral laws and election administration structures and the promotion of a sense of citizenship and its attendant rights and responsibilities. The recent experience of the United Nations in Nigeria shows how a partnership in electoral assistance can build a base for long-term post-electoral assistance activities.

111. The United Nations wealth of experience in electoral assistance allows the Organization to tailor its programmes to meet the particular demands of its Member States with great efficacy.

The United Nations, regional organizations and security

112. During the 1990s, regional organizations have played an increasingly active role in regional security affairs, not only in the realms of preventive diplomacy, peacekeeping and confidence-building, but also with respect to peace enforcement. The relationship between the United Nations and regional organizations is complex, usually fruitful, but sometimes difficult. Several lessons have emerged from recent experience.

113. First, it is imperative that regional security operations be mandated by the Security Council if the legal basis of the international security system is to be maintained. Frequently, such operations will also need the wider political support that only the United Nations can provide, and peace settlements will often require United Nations involvement under Security Council authority.

114. Second, security policies that work in one region may not in others. Most regions do not have organizations with the capacity to carry out major peacekeeping or peace enforcement operations. Some regional organizations—most notably OAU—would like to develop a peacekeeping capacity and it is important for the international community to assist them. This is a long-term undertaking, however, and one in which the parties can count on the United Nations to play an active supporting role.

115. Third, today's complex humanitarian emergencies require equally complex multidisciplinary responses, which only the United Nations has the qualifications and experience to provide. Whether responding to crises or implementing comprehensive peace agreements, the United Nations has an unparalleled ability to coordinate action across a wide range of sectors and disciplines.

116. I support moves towards greater cooperation with regional organizations. However, as multilateral activity expands, both the Secretariat and Member States are finding that the human and financial resources allotted for new operations have not kept pace with increased demands, and are at times barely adequate. It is crucial that this situation be addressed with energy and resolve if the United Nations is to avoid a cycle in which expectations exceed capacity, bringing inevitable disappointment and a decline in confidence in the potential of the Organization.

Disarmament

117. During the past year, existing disarmament agreements were threatened by a number of developments which are likely not only to undermine global security but also to cause an increase in global military expenditures. The disarmament machinery in the United Nations was not fully utilized during the year, and no consensus was reached on the convening of a fourth special session of the General Assembly devoted to disarmament, which could set universal goals for the immediate future. However, the United Nations has remained committed to upholding existing norms and to facilitating the necessary political will among Member States to establish new agreements to achieve global security at the lowest level of armaments commensurate with legitimate self-defence and security requirements.

118. The development of longer-range missiles and their testing by several countries, together with the development of missile defences and the fact that large numbers of missiles are ready to be launched on warning, seriously threaten peace and security. Multilaterally negotiated norms against the spread of ballistic missile technology for military purposes and restraint in missile development would considerably reduce the threat posed by ballistic missiles, whether armed with conventional weapons or capable of delivering weapons of mass destruction. Furthermore, they would substantially improve prospects for progress on bilateral and multilateral disarmament and arms control negotiations, including the prevention of an arms race in outer space.

119. The systematic and progressive reduction of nuclear weapons, with the ultimate goal of their complete elimination, will remain one of the priority tasks of the international community. Little was achieved in this area in the past year, however. Long-standing differences over how to tackle questions of nuclear disarmament continued to prevent the start of negotiations on a treaty banning the production of fissile material, which, in the autumn of 1998, had seemed possible. Meanwhile, we have continued to support ongoing negotiations on the establishment of a nuclear-weapon-free zone in Central Asia, and a text of the treaty is evolving.

120.   Efforts to promote entry into force of the Comprehensive Nuclear-Test-Ban Treaty continue, and a conference to consider the issue is scheduled for the autumn. It is crucial that the three nuclear-weapon States that have not yet ratified the Treaty, as well as those States whose ratification is required for its entry into force, deposit their instruments promptly. The path to the 2000 Review Conference of the Parties to the Treaty on the Non-Proliferation of Nuclear Weapons will be smoother if there has been tangible progress in this and other areas of nuclear disarmament.

121.   Disarmament activity—in the form of treaties, components of peacekeeping mandates or confidence-building measures—both supports, and is supported by, progress in social and economic development. Promotion of mine awareness, progress in mine clearance, and the provision of medical, psychological and technical assistance to mine victims, who are mainly women and children, sustain the process of socio-economic reconstruction and development in countries emerging from conflict. In May, the worldwide efforts to abolish landmines took a major step forward with the convening of the First Meeting of the States Parties to the Ottawa Convention, which bans anti-personnel mines and mandates their destruction. A further step towards reducing the devastation wrought by land-mines will be taken in December, when the parties to Amended Protocol II of the Convention on Certain Conventional Weapons, which constitutes a partial prohibition on landmines, will hold their first annual conference.

122. Other practical disarmament measures, such as the collection and destruction of small arms and light weapons, can reduce the potential for violence and enhance stability, thus facilitating the development process. The reduction of military budgets, especially in post-conflict countries, will increase the resources available for development. The latter issue will, we hope, be considered in depth by the re-established high-level Steering Group on Disarmament and Development.

123. The failure of the Conference on Disarmament, for the third year in succession, to agree on a programme of work and the lack of consensus on holding a special session of the General Assembly on disarmament are a source of grave and ongoing concern.

Sanctions

124. It is increasingly accepted that the design and implementation of sanctions mandated by the Security Council need to be improved, and their humanitarian costs to civilian populations reduced as far as possible. This can be achieved by more selective targeting of sanctions, as proponents of so-called "smart sanctions" have urged, or by incorporating appropriate and carefully thought through humanitarian exceptions directly in Security Council resolutions. I support both approaches.

125. Intense debate continues, both within and outside the United Nations, on how effective the existing sanctions regimes have been, whether comprehensive, like those against Iraq, or more targeted, as in the case of the Libyan Arab Jamahiriya. Questions remain on how best to address the problems arising from their application.

126. Since 1997, the Government of Switzerland has facilitated a dialogue between sanctions practitioners and experts, known as "the Interlaken process". Its goal has been to explore the potential effectiveness of targeted financial sanctions, which may include freezing the financial assets and blocking the financial transactions of targeted entities or individuals. Although their efficacy remains to be tested, and several issues require resolution, the technical feasibility of such sanctions has now been established, as reflected in a report submitted to the Security Council in June 1999.

2 Cooperating for development

Overview

127. In an increasingly interdependent world, the challenges of development can be met only through well-planned, coordinated and adequately funded international action. The United Nations and its partners have extraordinary capacities in the development field. The challenge is to use them more effectively and synergistically. In the reform programme I initiated in 1997, the United Nations Development Group was created to help meet this challenge. During the past year, the Group has been developing and implementing the new modes of collaboration necessary to meet our development goals.

Reform tools: common country assessment and United Nations Development Assistance Framework

128. Through the common country assessment and the United Nations Development Assistance Framework (UNDAF), the United Nations has for the first time the tools needed to provide strategic and coordinated support for the development goals of national Governments. The common country assessment provides a common analysis for use by the United Nations, donors and other institutions, so that all have a shared understanding of the challenges and potential risks they face. The United Nations Development Assistance Framework is the planning and programming mechanism that coordinates the United Nations response to meeting these challenges.

129. We are also taking steps to ensure that those United Nations programmes, funds and agencies, including the regional commissions, that do not have a presence in the field are fully involved in the preparation and implementation of United Nations Development Assistance Frameworks and common country assessments. Since 1997, some 60 countries have initiated common country assessments; 18 countries participated in the UNDAF pilot project started in 1997, and 19 more are expected to commence an UNDAF before the end of 1999.

Strengthening leadership: the resident coordinator system

130. Throughout the last year, the United Nations Development Group has intensified efforts to improve the resident coordinator system. These have included new selection procedures for resident coordinators to broaden the basis for recruitment and improve the gender balance; performance appraisals of resident coordinators and country teams; improved annual reporting procedures for resident coordinators and a review of lessons learned; and greater support from Headquarters, including better training for resident coordinators and country teams.

Maximizing resources: harmonization and United Nations Houses

131. In response to a call by the General Assembly for greater harmonization and simplification of the policies and procedures used by United Nations bodies, 100 country teams have now planned to have their individual pro-

gramming cycles begin at the same time, and all country programmes will have harmonized cycles by 2004.

132. The housing of United Nations entities in common premises (United Nations Houses) will foster a greater sense of community and common purpose. To date, some 36 United Nations Houses have been designated around the world; the establishment of 20 more is being considered in 1999. In a number of countries, we are promoting "virtual" United Nations Houses that will connect separate offices via an in-country intranet and thus improve the sharing of information, practices and expertise.

Improving impact: inter-agency support

133. The United Nations Development Group has set up a number of inter-agency groups to provide support to country teams. The Working Group on the Right to Development reviewed the provisional UNDAF guidelines and made specific proposals on how better to incorporate respect for human rights. The Working Group prepared a guidance note for all resident coordinators and will develop a human rights training module. The Group will also disseminate examples of good practice to help country teams learn from each other.

134. The Sub-Group on Gender, formed in June 1998, reviewed the pilot United Nations Development Assistance Frameworks and made recommendations for more effective incorporation of gender perspectives into the core indicators of the common country assessments and the final UNDAF guidelines.

135. Ad hoc task forces and working groups have pooled knowledge gained by the United Nations Development Group on specific topics for the benefit of country teams. In 1998/99, these included the Working Groups on

poverty and girls' education, and the Task Forces on globalization, sector programmes and collaboration with the Bretton Woods institutions.

Working together: building partnerships for development

136. During the past year, the United Nations placed greater emphasis on communicating its research, publications and debates to its various partners—nationally, regionally and internationally. This has contributed to greater understanding and awareness of key development issues and to more innovative development thinking. In addition, a database set up jointly by the United Nations Children's Fund (UNICEF), the United Nations Population Fund (UNFPA) and UNDP has deepened mutual understanding and provided valuable input for civil society organizations. A survey carried out by the World Food Programme (WFP) in 1998 found that WFP is collaborating with more than 1,100 non-governmental organizations worldwide, of which three quarters are national and local groups.

137. In response to my statement to business leaders at the World Economic Forum at Davos in 1999, the United Nations Development Group has explored private sector partnerships on a range of development issues. UNDP, for example, has joined with Internet giant Cisco Systems in creating NetAid, a multi-city concert to be broadcast over the Internet to raise public awareness and generate financial support for reducing poverty in developing countries. UNICEF's partnerships with the private sector include a global campaign that has succeeded in eliminating polio in many parts of the world.

138. The United Nations has also made concerted efforts to increase collaboration with the international financial institutions. In February 1999, the Economic and Social Council held a high-level meeting with the Executive Board members of the World Bank and the International Monetary Fund (IMF). Top World Bank officials, including President Wolfensohn and 11 Vice-Presidents, have participated in other exchanges, in the General Assembly, the Economic and Social Council and various open meetings. Discussions have also been held with World Bank officials on the Comprehensive Development Framework and other areas for cooperation, such as the common country assessment and UNDAF. Within the United Nations, including the specialized agencies, there have been a number of discussions on how to make United Nations engagement with the World Bank more effective. The United Nations has also collaborated actively with the regional development banks, particularly in regard to the financial crises in East Asia and elsewhere. Similarly, there has been practical collaboration at the country level and in following up UNDAF/Country Assistance Strategy pilots in Mali and Viet Nam.

139. The United Nations has continued to stress that governance grounded in democracy, the rule of law and respect for human rights is the best foundation for sustainable development. Cooperation has increased markedly between the Office of the United Nations High Commissioner for Human Rights, UNDP, the international financial institutions and the specialized agencies on integrating human rights norms into the development process. The next stage will be to draw upon the practical experiences of Governments throughout the world to identify where, and what sort of, assistance is most needed.

The link between relief and development

140. Inter-agency task forces engaged in post-conflict peace-building have become increasingly common in the 1990s as the number of comprehensive peace agreements has grown. This development has highlighted the need to ensure that emergency relief and recovery assistance programmes are linked effectively to longer-term development initiatives. Recognizing the importance of this linkage, we have initiated a dialogue between the principal actors in the humanitarian, human rights, security and development fields; its goal is to facilitate more effective interdepartmental and inter-agency cooperation. The first meeting of the Executive Committees on Peace and Security, Political Affairs and the United Nations Development Group in November 1998 was an important step in this process.

Capacity-building in statistics

141. In May 1998, the Economic and Social Council, recognizing the importance of statistics and indicators, requested the United Nations Secretariat, bilateral funding agencies and the Bretton Woods institutions to work together to provide support for national statistical capacity-building in Member States. The Department of Economic and Social Affairs, in collaboration with UNFPA, has undertaken various initiatives to implement the 2000 world population and housing census. The Department has also supported regional approaches for census-taking in Central Asia, the Southern African Development Community and the Pacific. Intraregional cooperation among organizations responsible for collecting national and regional statistics is also being supported.

Eradication of poverty

142. Despite improvements over the past 50 years in nutrition, health, education and life expectancy and in reducing material poverty, we still have far to travel: over 1.5 billion people live on less than $1 a day; almost 1 billion adults—a majority of them women—are unable to read or write; 830 million people are malnourished; and 750 million people have no access to adequate shelter or health care. Gender inequalities continue to hamper economic growth and well-being.

143. Increased natural disasters, the hangover from the East Asian economic crisis, the continuing economic decline of the former Soviet Union, the growing toll of AIDS, especially in Africa, and new outbreaks of war have exacerbated poverty in many parts of the world in 1998.

144. The eradication of poverty is one of the central goals of the United Nations and its agencies, but its achievement remains elusive. While declining aid flows are part of the problem, increasing aid is not a panacea. In some cases, aid has made a real difference in reducing poverty; in others, it has made little or no impact. What makes the difference is how the aid is used. Where foreign assistance is misused, it is of little benefit to those in need.

145. The United Nations has long recognized that development policy is about more than economics narrowly defined. Development cannot occur in a vacuum. It requires that minimal levels of human security are met and that there is inclusive political participation and respect for human rights. As the only international organization with a mandate that embraces security, development and human rights, the United Nations is uniquely well placed to tackle the eradication of poverty in a holistic manner. This requires broad inter-agency cooperation, which is increasingly common practice in today's United Nations. For example, work carried out jointly by the International Labour Organization (ILO), the Department of Economic and Social Affairs, UNDP, the World Bank and IMF formed the basis for my report to the Economic and Social Council in July 1999 on the role of employment and work in poverty eradication: the empowerment and advancement of women.

146. Better poverty eradication policy requires improved risk assessment and early warning strategies—as have been developed jointly by the International Fund for Agricultural Development, FAO and WFP. More generally over the past year, the United Nations has been working with its partners to produce more holistic development policies. The Administrative Committee on Coordination sent an action plan, entitled "Freedom from poverty" and based on its statement on poverty of March 1998, to all United Nations resident coordinators and country teams in October 1998. The plan forms the basis for a new initiative, led by the United Nations Development Group, to help programme countries to meet the goal of halving absolute poverty by 2015.

147. In December 1998, the United Nations Development Group developed an action plan for country-level responses to the challenges of globalization and the financial crisis in East Asia. Seventy-eight countries have either developed a separate strategy for poverty reduction (43 countries) or dedicated part of their overall development plan to poverty reduction (35 countries). United Nations country teams have established inter-agency thematic working groups on gender (in 58 countries), food security (in 48 countries) and a range of other issues related to poverty eradication. In 1998, the Economic and Social Commission

for Western Asia (ESCWA), drawing on studies carried out in 1996/97, began to develop poverty alleviation policies.

148. By the end of 1998, the Poverty Strategies Initiative of UNDP had provided support to over 100 countries in the area of poverty analysis, mapping and monitoring and developing national poverty reduction strategies. This initiative involved extensive collaboration at the country level with the World Bank, the regional commissions, ILO, UNICEF, the Department of Economic and Social Affairs and UNFPA.

149. The United Nations Development Fund for Women (UNIFEM) and UNDP initiated a global knowledge network designed to help produce effective pro-poor budgets that were also sensitive to gender and environmental concerns. WFP assisted almost 75 million people, more than half of them women and children, helping to build sustainable food security assets for the poor and responding to their needs in emergency situations. A UNFPA study in South-East Asia on the effects of the financial crisis revealed increasing poverty in the region, and recommended specific policy responses.

150. In May 1999, the United Nations Centre for Human Settlements (Habitat) and the World Bank launched the Cities Alliance to coordinate their support for cities in the developing world. The Alliance focuses in particular on urban squatters, upgrading slums and improving urban governance and management systems. UNDP, with support from Habitat, the United Nations Industrial Development Organization, the United Nations Educational, Scientific and Cultural Organization (UNESCO) and the United Nations Conference on Trade and Development (UNCTAD), launched the World Alliance of Cities against Poverty as follow-up to the Habitat II process.

151. The United Nations International Drug Control Programme has helped Governments in Latin America and Asia develop "business plans" to reduce incentives for the cultivation of illicit drugs and promote alternative development activities. Meanwhile, United Nations agencies have continued their collaboration with civil society organizations with a view to achieving one of the goals of the Microcredit Summit, namely, to provide 100 million of the poorest families with access to credit and other financial services.

Social development

152. One of the most significant achievements of the international conferences on social development issues convened by the United Nations during the 1990s has been the consensus on the need for people-centred approaches to both social and economic problems. In 1999, the five-year review of the International Conference on Population and Development, held at Cairo in 1994, was conducted in New York. Preparatory work also began for the five-year reviews, to be held in 2000, of the Fourth World Conference on Women and the World Summit for Social Development, and of Habitat II, which will occur in 2001.

153. The review process of the Cairo Conference culminated in a special session of the General Assembly, held from 30 June to 2 July 1999, at which the Assembly adopted key actions for the further implementation of the Programme of Action of the International Conference on Population and Development. This drew on reports prepared by the Department of Economic and Social Affairs on the basis of several technical workshops and symposia, and an on-the-ground assessment of progress made in 114 developing countries and 18 developed countries since the Cairo

Conference. The document adopted by the General Assembly focused on population and development concerns; gender equity and the empowerment of women; reproductive health and rights; partnerships and collaborations. It also called for a greater effort by all countries to address the shortfall in resources needed to implement the commitments made at Cairo.

154. At the country level, inter-agency working groups have been established to assist with the integrated follow-up to the conferences. The 1998 annual reports of resident coordinators indicated that 573 thematic groups were functioning around the world. Many of these groups deal with social development concerns, such as basic social services (16 groups), health and nutrition (29), education (24), population and development (7), reproductive health (5), drugs (6) and human rights (15).

155. The use of new information technologies has assisted public information outreach on social development issues. For example, in March 1999 the UNIFEM inter-agency global videoconference, *A World Free of Violence against Women*, linked Member States, United Nations bodies and activists around the world.

156. In addition, ESCWA is implementing a project to provide an integrated regional follow-up by the Arab States to the United Nations conferences, which was launched in October 1998. The project addresses issues related to the themes of the major conferences, including women, population, human settlements and social development. The project also builds on the experiences of UNICEF, UNFPA and UNIFEM.

157. Four particular areas of activity are highlighted below.

A new initiative for girls' education

158. Led by UNICEF, the United Nations Development Group is planning to launch a new 10-year initiative for girls' education. The initiative will bring together a broad coalition of actors, including those outside the United Nations system, to support enhanced provision of girls' education at country level. The Conferences on Population and Development and on Women, and the Social Summit, have demonstrated widespread recognition of the benefits that enhancing the education of girls confers, including increased family incomes, later marriages and reduced fertility rates, reduced infant and maternal mortality rates, better nourished and healthier children, greater opportunities and choices for more women, and greater participation of women in development and in political and economic decision-making.

Focus on youth

159. Contributing to young people's development has important implications for human development and human rights, including strengthening democratic processes and decreasing gender and ethnic discrimination and disparities. The United Nations has continued to build partnerships and strengthen its commitment to supporting young people around the world. In 10 United Nations country teams, inter-agency working groups have been established on children, youth and adolescents.

160. The United Nations International Drug Control Programme sponsored a Youth Vision Drug Abuse Forum bringing together young people from around the world to exchange ideas on tackling drug-related problems. The General Assembly at its special session on the world drug

problem agreed on the importance of reducing the demand for drugs as well as cutting off the supply. The World AIDS Campaign focused on young people in both 1998 and 1999.

161. UNIFEM, UNFPA, UNDP and UNESCO, in partnership with civil society organizations, sponsored the Global Meeting of Generations initiative that fosters dialogue between generations to further human development in the twenty-first century. UNICEF, with the support of the Rockefeller Foundation and the United Nations Foundation, collaborated with a number of United Nations and non-governmental organization partners to develop and support interregional dialogues aimed at formulating policies and programmes which take account of the needs of young people. UNFPA continued to foster regional and national cooperation in adolescent reproductive health by sponsoring a number of events in the Caribbean, sub-Saharan Africa, Asia and the Arab States.

Advocating higher and more focused social spending

162. The 20/20 initiative, by which recipient countries agree to dedicate 20 per cent of their national budgets—and donors give 20 per cent of their development assistance—to social development spending, has drawn attention to the need to increase spending on social development priorities and has stimulated debate on donor and in-country policies. UNICEF, UNDP, UNFPA and the World Bank collaborated both at the international level and in specific countries on this issue over the past year, building on work begun after the Social Summit.

163. Thirty-five social sector expenditure reviews have been completed to date. In October 1998, at the sec-

ond international meeting on the 20/20 initiative, representatives from 48 countries adopted the Hanoi consensus, which emphasizes the need for increased investment
in social services.

United Nations collaboration in the fight against HIV/AIDS

164. The challenge posed by the global AIDS epi-
demic is growing increasingly serious. By the end of 1998,
over 30 million people were infected by HIV/AIDS and almost 14 million had succumbed to the disease. Half of the
6 million new cases of HIV infection in 1998 were young
people aged 15 to 24. According to the *World Health Report 1999*, AIDS is now the most deadly infectious disease
in the world, killing even more people than tuberculosis.

165. In a number of poor countries, HIV/AIDS is having a major negative impact on progress towards achieving
social development goals. For example, according to a report produced by the Department of Economic and Social
Affairs in 1998, the nine countries most affected by AIDS
will have experienced a 10-year reduction in life expectancy by the year 2000, and a 16-year reduction by
2010-2015. By 2005-2010, infant mortality in the most affected countries could be 28 per cent higher than it would
have been in the absence of AIDS, and mortality under age
5 could be 51 per cent higher. Social and economic losses
create a downward spiral, reversing hard-won development gains and depriving those infected of any chance of a
decent livelihood.

166. In 1998, the United Nations International Drug
Control Programme became the seventh sponsor of the
Joint and Co-sponsored United Nations Programme on
HIV/AIDS (UNAIDS), joining UNICEF, UNDP, UNFPA,

UNESCO, the World Health Organization (WHO) and the World Bank. UNAIDS achievements include the production of a series of guides to the strategic planning process for national responses to HIV/AIDS (with UNAIDS support, 13 countries in Asia and Africa have now completed their strategic plans); the publication of over 100 guides to best practices, which include advocacy material, technical updates and case studies; preparations for a new International Partnership against HIV/AIDS in Africa; the establishment of an inter-agency working group on HIV/AIDS with the participation of 115 United Nations country teams; and the launch of a joint initiative by UNAIDS, UNIFEM and UNFPA to build the capacity of women's organizations and Governments to address the challenges of HIV/AIDS.

Sustainable development

167. The seventh session of the Commission on Sustainable Development in 1999 attracted a record number of ministerial participants, confirming the role of the Commission as the main high-level intergovernmental forum on sustainable development. Participants agreed to address the most pressing problems of sustainable development and management of the world's oceans and seas; to promote sustainable development in tourism; and to encourage further action to achieve more sustainable production and consumption. In addition, the five-year review of progress on the Barbados Programme of Action for the Sustainable Development of Small Island Developing States, which represent more than one fifth of the membership of the United Nations, will be held in September 1999.

168. The United Nations Development Group and other bodies in the United Nations system have continued to work together on sustainable development and environmental issues. In January 1999, the United Nations Environment Programme (UNEP) and Habitat, in collaboration with UNDP and the World Bank, launched a joint regional initiative to improve water management in African cities. The Office to Combat Desertification and Drought continues to provide assistance to a number of countries. To date, 49 countries have benefited.

169. The United Nations Revolving Fund for Natural Resources Exploration promoted environment-friendly mining activities in Mozambique and Suriname and distributed guidebooks on CD-ROM to over 50 countries. In 1998, UNDP completed 75 conversion projects in 19 countries under the Montreal Protocol, which supports the conversion of contaminated industrial sites into usable, safe land. The Office of the United Nations High Commissioner for Refugees (UNHCR) and WFP together identified sustainable environmental management practices in areas hosting large numbers of refugees. ESCWA continued to work towards developing environmental indicators for the Arab region.

170. In 1998, the Department of Economic and Social Affairs, the World Energy Council and UNDP jointly launched the world energy assessment to provide background scientific and technical data for bodies involved in furthering the work of Agenda 21. Through their partnership in the Global Environment Facility (GEF), UNDP, UNEP and the World Bank have helped 138 countries to prepare national strategies to implement their commitments under the United Nations Framework Convention on Climate Change and the Convention on Biological Diversity.

171. Reform of the United Nations Secretariat has improved user access to the analytical and technical work of the Department of Economic and Social Affairs. This in

turn will help ensure that the results of policy deliberations in intergovernmental forums, particularly the Commission on Sustainable Development, contribute more effectively to United Nations support for national sustainable
development policies.

Africa

172. Working with national and regional partners to
improve the lives of people in Africa remains a priority for
the United Nations Development Group. The challenges
are clear. An estimated 44 per cent of Africans, and 51 per
cent of those in sub-Saharan Africa, are living in absolute
poverty. Of the 30 million people infected by HIV/AIDS in
the world, 23 million live in sub-Saharan Africa; 91 per cent
of all AIDS deaths in the world have occurred in 34 countries—29 of which are in Africa. If Africa is to reach the Social Summit's target of halving absolute poverty by 2015,
annual GDP must rise by at least 7 per cent until 2015.
Growth is currently around 3 per cent and is expected to
reach 3.5 per cent in 2000. Africa's debt burden increased
from $344 billion in 1997 to $350 billion in 1998, a sum
equivalent to 300 per cent of exports of goods and services.
Africa received less than $5 billion in foreign direct invest-
ment, a mere 3 per cent of global flows.

Enhancing United Nations collaboration for the development of Africa

173. I presented my report on the causes of conflict
and the promotion of durable peace and sustainable development in Africa to the Economic and Social Council at its
substantive session of 1999. It highlighted the need for

substantial and sustained economic growth and social development to meet the challenges faced by African countries. Against this background, the United Nations Development Group, with some of the Executive Committees, has developed an action plan to identify common activities and the most appropriate contributions from individual agencies.

174. The Administrative Committee on Coordination continues to stress the need to tie United Nations initiatives in Africa—the United Nations New Agenda for the Development of Africa in the 1990s and its implementing arm, the United Nations System-wide Special Initiative—into other development undertakings, such as the Tokyo International Conference on African Development, the Heavily Indebted Poor Countries Debt Initiative, the Alliance for African Industrialization and the coordinated follow-up to the United Nations conferences. The first annual regional coordination meeting of the United Nations system in Africa was held at Nairobi in March 1999, chaired by the Deputy Secretary-General. It adopted the System-wide Special Initiative and the New Agenda as the framework for coordinating the United Nations approach to the development of Africa.

175. Under the auspices of the United Nations Development Group, 10 African countries have participated in the UNDAF pilot phase. Ten more UNDAFs are expected in Africa by the end of 1999 in preparation for the programme cycles beginning in 2001.

Tackling the challenges of poverty in Africa

176. The Jobs for Africa programme is an integral part of the System-wide Special Initiative and meets commitments made at the Social Summit. It aims to develop and strengthen the capacity of national and regional institutions and networks in 10 participating countries to combat poverty by generating productive employment. Following up on the Summit and taking on the fight against poverty was also the topic for a subregional meeting organized by the Economic Commission for Africa (ECA) in March 1999.

177. The United Nations Development Programme has sponsored a number of long-term national studies to enable Governments to define objectives for poverty eradication, taking into account the effects of globalization and investment flows. A regional decision-making information system was set up in Zimbabwe in 1999 with outreach to other African countries. The programme has benefited 14 countries to date, and another 30 have made formal requests for support.

178. The Africa 2000 initiative of UNDP, providing support to rural women in Africa for sustainable development activities, had sponsored over 700 projects by the end of 1998. At a cost of $1.5 billion, WFP is providing assistance to approximately 21 million people in Africa through 100 projects. In southern Africa, WFP has been working with national partners through its vulnerability analysis and mapping units to promote the use of vulnerability monitoring and analysis to develop contingency plans for tackling regional natural disasters.

179. The United Nations Centre for Human Settlements established the African Forum on Urban Poverty in September 1998. Its Urban Management Programme, supported by UNDP and the World Bank, already covers 26 African countries. The Sustainable Cities Programme, implemented jointly with UNEP, operates in eight African countries.

Focusing on health and education for Africa

180. Led by UNESCO, UNICEF and the World Bank, education activities under the Special Initiative focused during the year on improving primary education in 16 countries where primary school enrolment is low. United Nations agencies were also involved in improving the quality of education in Cameroon, Côte d'Ivoire, Ethiopia, Madagascar, Malawi, Uganda and the United Republic of Tanzania.

181. UNAIDS, together with its sponsors (UNICEF, UNDP, UNFPA, UNESCO, WHO, the World Bank and the United Nations International Drug Control Programme), intensified its campaign against HIV and AIDS in Africa. Seeking as broad a base as possible for its campaign, UNAIDS has brought together Governments, regional bodies, bilateral development agencies, multilateral organizations and the corporate sector, with commitments from large pharmaceutical corporations, the entertainment industry and the Global Business Council on AIDS, as well as civil society organizations.

182. Africa, whose peoples are major victims of malaria, is a principal beneficiary of the WHO-led Roll Back Malaria campaign, which aims to cut deaths from malaria by 50 per cent by 2010 and 75 per cent by 2015. Other United Nations initiatives, such as National Immunization Days, have also helped women and children in many African countries.

183. The work of UNFPA in assisting countries in Africa to implement the Programme of Action of the International Conference on Population and Development has led to concrete improvement in reproductive health care in 19 countries. Four countries have introduced legislation outlawing the practice of female genital mutilation.

184. A major focus of the development activities of WFP is on enhancing women's capacity to increase household food security.

Building national capacity for good governance and trade

185. Collaboration with national, regional and international partners in Africa is central to the United Nations efforts to strengthen national capacity for good governance and trade. The Special Initiative governance group established the Africa Governance Forum and is creating comprehensive databases to analyse government practices. The Forum met in June 1999 in Mali to examine the link between governance and conflict management. In addition, UNIFEM's programme on governance and leadership is promoting greater gender balance in decision-making by voters, candidates and elected representatives in Africa.

186. UNDP, together with UNCTAD, UNIDO, UNESCO, the World Trade Organization (WTO), the African Development Bank, OAU and ECA, organized a forum in March 1999 to consider how to create a positive environment for investment and to enhance competitiveness.

187. The Special Initiative trade group, led by UNCTAD in collaboration with WTO and the International Trade Centre, has developed an integrated framework for trade-related technical assistance. The UNCTAD Asia-Africa Business Networking Forum (March 1999) is itself an example of the continuing United Nations support for South-South cooperation.

United Nations Fund for International Partnerships

188. Since the establishment of the United Nations Fund for International Partnerships in March 1998, four funding rounds have been completed and almost $140 million awarded to 79 projects covering population and women (33 projects), children's health (15 projects), environment (20 projects) and selected United Nations causes (11 projects) which include the provision of support to the Secretary-General's reform programme. Funds have also been earmarked for emergency assistance relief efforts to the Kosovo region.

189. At the beginning of 1999, a more streamlined and efficient funding process was launched. Separate "programme framework groups" were established to provide guidance for the preparation of specific projects. The groups include population and women, focusing particularly on adolescent girls and the quality of reproductive health services; children's health, focusing particularly on decreasing childhood mortality and reducing smoking; and the environment, focusing particularly on biodiversity and energy and climate change.

3 Meeting humanitarian commitments

190. The past year was fraught with humanitarian disasters. The extraordinary rise in the number and scale of natural disasters was particularly striking. New armed conflicts broke out with enormous loss of life, massive forced displacement and human suffering in Eritrea, Ethiopia and the southern Balkans, while protracted emergencies continued in Afghanistan, Angola, Sierra Leone, the Sudan and elsewhere.

191. Timely humanitarian action in many countries continued to be compromised by the deliberate targeting of civilians and humanitarian workers and denial of access to humanitarian assistance. Responding to this unacceptable flouting of humanitarian norms, the Security Council initiated a series of open debates on the protection of civilians in armed conflict.

Coordinating humanitarian action

192. The Office for the Coordination of Humanitarian Affairs has continued to strengthen its three core functions: coordination of humanitarian action, policy development and humanitarian advocacy.

193. Coordination efforts focused on improving the environment for humanitarian action in a number of ways, including negotiation with parties to conflicts over access and security; reinforcement of the principles of humanitarian action; and advocacy with the Security Council and other bodies. The need for greater respect for, adherence to and application of international laws and norms relating to the rights of civilians has been a central focus in this year of the fiftieth anniversary of the Geneva Conventions. In January and February 1999, the Security Council held two open sessions on this issue. The resulting presidential statement requested that I submit a report on the protection of civilians to the Security Council in September 1999, identifying innovative ways in which the Council, acting within its mandate, could strengthen its capacity to ensure the protection of civilians in conflict.

194. For the first time, the consolidated inter-agency appeals were launched simultaneously (in December 1998 for 1999). As at 31 July, the response to the appeals was about 49 per cent of the amount sought. Excluding southeastern Europe, however, the response was 31.6 per cent, only marginally better than in 1998. The geographical and sectoral commitment of funds has been extremely uneven, meaning that not even minimum levels of assistance could be guaranteed in certain sectors and that some countries were left critically underfunded. The poor response to crises in Africa, at a time when many donor countries are enjoying a period of prolonged prosperity, was particularly distressing.

195. Effective coordination is particularly important in designing the inter-agency response to the needs of internally displaced persons, since there is no single international lead agency. Work carried out jointly by my Special Representative for internally displaced persons, the Office of the United Nations High Commissioner for Human Rights and the Office for the Coordination of Humanitarian Affairs has formed the basis for a policy paper of the Inter-Agency Standing Committee, which will soon be finalized, on protection of internally displaced persons. It identifies ways of ensuring that protection responsibilities are discharged effectively and sets out a system that can rapidly assign responsibilities to different agencies in emergency situations. Other initiatives during the past year included the undertaking of a review of country situations affected by internal displacement, the preparation of a compendium of good field practice and the development of a global database of internally displaced persons.

196. As the number of major natural and environmental disasters has increased, efforts to enhance the coordination of United Nations responses to them have included the launch of three major inter-agency appeals—for hurricane Mitch and for the floods in Bangladesh and China. In addition, 17 United Nations disaster assessment and coordination teams were dispatched during the year. Situation reports on over 60 natural disasters were disseminated. Twenty-eight international appeals were launched, and over $1 billion was raised. The Office for the Coordination of Humanitarian Affairs and UNDP jointly organized an international disaster management workshop in Beijing in June 1999 to examine ways of enhancing response-preparedness and capacity-building and bridging the gap between emergency relief and early recovery. Regional workshops and seminars were also held. These focused on the development of contingency plans and the strengthening of disaster assessment and coordination teams in disaster-prone regions.

197. A series of thematic events and regional conferences was organized to mark the end of the International Decade for Natural Disaster Reduction. This culminated in a programme forum, held at Geneva in July 1999 and involving all partners in the Framework of Action for the Decade. A comprehensive disaster reduction strategy for the twenty-first century was adopted by the forum, and reviewed by the Economic and Social Council. The latter evaluated the achievements of the Decade and adopted a resolution to ensure continuation of United Nations multisectoral and concerted disaster reduction activities in the future.

198. The Executive Committee on Humanitarian Affairs, under the chairmanship of the Emergency Relief Coordinator, has achieved greater synergy in dealing with issues that have strong security, peacekeeping and political implications for humanitarian assistance. FAO and WHO have recently been invited to participate in the meetings of the Executive Committee. The Inter-Agency Standing Committee remained the principal forum for inter-agency coordination, consultation and decision-making on humanitarian issues.

199. The Inter-Agency Standing Committee has set up working groups on a number of issues. These include natural disasters, improving the consolidated appeal process, human rights and humanitarian action, internally displaced persons, gender and humanitarian response, training, small arms, assistance to countries in the Commonwealth of Independent States, post-conflict reintegration and millennium initiatives. The admission of the World Bank as a member in March 1999 has further strengthened the effectiveness of the Committee. Major priority has also been given to strengthening the systems for coordination in the field, particularly the capacity of humanitarian coordinators, through, for example, the joint consultation of resident and humanitarian coordinators that was held in December 1998. Generic guidelines for strategic frameworks have also been developed from work piloted in Afghanistan.

Delivering humanitarian services

200. In the past year, the United Nations assisted countries and regions affected by over 60 natural disasters, as well as by man-made emergencies. These included Afghanistan, Angola, Armenia, Azerbaijan, Burundi, the Republic of the Congo, the Democratic Republic of the Congo, the Democratic People's Republic of Korea, Eritrea, Ethiopia, Georgia, Guinea-Bissau, Liberia, the Russian Federation, Rwanda, Sierra Leone, Somalia, the Sudan, Tajikistan, Uganda, the former Yugoslavia and the Great Lakes region of Africa. This assistance has often involved innovative joint initiatives. Some examples are the collaboration on health issues between the Pan American Health Organization and UNICEF against cholera in Central America; initiatives undertaken by UNHCR and UNICEF in West Africa on child soldiers and unaccompanied children; and initiatives on gender by UNICEF and WFP.

201. Attacks on humanitarian personnel continued to pose major problems. In 1998, 22 United Nations staff members and many more local and international personnel from non-governmental organizations involved in complex emergencies lost their lives. The loss of humanitarian personnel in several direct attacks in Angola and Somalia illustrated the growing extent of this problem. The World Food Programme lost 12 staff members in 1998. As a result, it has sought to improve staff security by providing at least three days of basic security awareness training for all agency personnel and making key improvements in the security of field facilities.

202. Disbursements of food aid increased in 1998. WFP assisted nearly 75 million people, with contributions amounting to $1.7 billion in 1998, a 33 per cent increase over 1997. In recognition of the challenges posed by its increased involvement in relief assistance, WFP established the Protracted Relief and Recovery Operation, a programme aimed at ensuring a seamless transition from emergency relief and life-saving activities to post-crisis recovery.

203. The health assistance programmes of WHO focused on assessing the health needs of those affected by emergencies and disasters, providing health information, assisting in health sector coordination and planning and implementing priority programmes in areas such as mental health, control of epidemics, immunization, pharmaceuticals and nutrition. Priority was given to strengthening the coordination between national health authorities and the international community, as well as to bridging the gap between recovery, rehabilitation and health development activities. Special efforts were made to eradicate polio and to control malaria in countries affected by emergencies, to improve health systems in the Palestinian self-rule areas, and to observe the equitable distribution of commodities imported under Security Council resolution 986 (1995) and the rehabilitation of health services in Iraq.

204. Humanitarian conventions are increasingly flouted in modern warfare, and children are major victims. In addressing the needs of children in conflict, UNICEF has continued to press for commitments from Governments and military bodies to act more effectively to protect children. It has urged an end to the use of child soldiers and the universal adoption of the global ban on anti-personnel landmines. Its in-country programmes to protect children in conflict zones have included mine-awareness programmes, and the negotiation of ceasefire agreements to allow the provision of food or immunization to those in need.

205. My Special Representative for Children and Armed Conflict has been working to increase global awareness of the impact of conflict on children and to mobilize the political support of both Governments and civil society to strengthen the protection, rights and welfare of children in armed conflict and its aftermath. At the country level, he undertook a series of visits to countries in, or affected by, armed conflict and sought to obtain commitments from the parties to conflicts and other key actors to providing better protection and welfare for children. Efforts are also under way to promote the inclusion of the protection and needs of children in peace processes, targeting several countries that are undergoing peace-building efforts. In August 1999, the Security Council adopted a resolution stressing the need for greater and more effective efforts to protect children in armed conflicts.

206. In recognizing children and women as bearers of rights who may play a central role in peace-building efforts, UNICEF has contributed to developing and conducting children's rights and gender awareness training for peacekeeping forces. As disasters and crises can affect women and men differently, the Inter-Agency Standing Committee has also developed a common policy on the integration of a gender perspective into humanitarian assistance programmes.

207. The majority of those affected by disasters live in the countryside. Here, FAO has played an important role in assessing damage to local production capacities, providing early warning of impending food emergencies, producing information on crop and food supplies and rendering technical advice to the numerous actors involved in agricultural emergency assistance. FAO has also provided considerable support to disaster-stricken farmers, helping to bridge the gap between relief and rehabilitation.

208. Many of today's gravest humanitarian crises are exacerbated by the use of mines, which in many areas continue to pose deadly threats to civilians long after hostilities have ceased. Responding to the threats posed by landmines, the Mine Action Service of the Department of Peacekeeping Operations has coordinated a number of inter-agency assessment missions, which have defined the problems and challenges facing individual countries and communities and proposed common and comprehensive responses. In addition, it has worked with its partners to develop and implement programmes in mine awareness, victim assistance, mine clearance and advocacy. These and other activities have been strongly supported by Member States, both through contributions to the Voluntary Trust Fund for Mine Action and through the many ratifications of the Ottawa Convention, which allowed it to enter into force on 1 March 1999.

209. The humanitarian community increasingly recognizes that it is part of its responsibility to ensure that relief programmes pave the way for sustainable development. UNDP and humanitarian agencies are working together to ensure that a concern for long-term sustainable human development informs relief operations. Programmes for the demobilization of former combatants, comprehensive mine action, the return and reintegration of refugees and internally displaced persons and the restoration of the institutions of good governance reflect this concern.

210. The United Nations Relief and Works Agency for Palestine Refugees in the Near East (UNRWA) combines humanitarian and development objectives in providing relief and social services to approximately 3.6 million Palestine refugees. A special feature of the Agency's operations has been its ability to maintain essential services, often on an emergency basis, in war and conflict situations. However, the Agency's continuing financial deficit, which reached $70 million against its 1999 budget of $322 million, has inevitably had a negative effect on the level and standard of services.

Assisting refugees

211. By the end of 1998, there were 21.4 million refugees and persons of concern to UNHCR compared with 22.3 million in 1997. Just over half (11.4 million) were refugees; the remainder comprised internally displaced persons, returnees, asylum-seekers and stateless people. The vast majority of refugees and persons of concern were in Africa, Asia and Europe.

212. In contrast to previous years, there were no large refugee movements in 1998 or in the beginning of 1999. Though numerous, the emergencies the humanitarian community dealt with were relatively small in size and of low visibility. This pattern changed dramatically in the last week of March 1999. From then, over the next three months, 850,000 Kosovar Albanians were forced from their homes—one of the largest and most rapid refugee exoduses of modern times. UNHCR and its partners, with the logistical support of the North Atlantic Treaty Organization, mounted a huge relief operation to assist those who streamed into Albania, the former Yugoslav Republic of Macedonia and Montenegro. More than 90,000 refugees were moved to countries in Europe and beyond under the auspices of the humanitarian evacuation programme. When peace was restored to Kosovo, the refugees returned almost as suddenly and in as large numbers as they had left. In just two weeks, more than 400,000 refugees crossed back into Kosovo.

213. The Kosovo crisis provides a graphic example of the close relationship between human rights abuses, war and refugee flows. The humanitarian and human rights communities both increasingly accept that responses to humanitarian crises must also tackle human rights failings. In Kosovo, the United Nations High Commissioner for Human Rights broke new ground by dispatching envoys to gather information about human rights violations and establishing field offices expressly for this purpose.

214. Africa provides many more tragic examples. The crises in Guinea-Bissau and Sierra Leone forced hundreds of thousands to flee their homes. Renewed fighting in the Democratic Republic of the Congo not only provoked new movements of refugees and displaced persons, but also made it extremely hazardous for humanitarian agencies to continue to provide relief. Late in 1998, the armed conflict between Eritrea and Ethiopia led to a new spate of displacement and mass expulsions in the Horn of Africa, while the internal war in the Republic of the Congo impelled 25,000 Congolese refugees from the Pool region to cross into Bas-Congo in the Democratic Republic of the Congo.

215. There was only limited voluntary repatriation in 1998. Ethiopian refugees were able to return from the Sudan; refugees returned from Ethiopia to north-west Somalia, indicating the restoration of some degree of peace and stability to at least parts of the Horn of Africa. In West Africa, the repatriation of Tuareg refugees to Mali and the Niger was completed, while sizeable numbers of Liberians returned home, either spontaneously (160,000 refugees) or with UNHCR assistance (110,000 since 1997). In Central America, long-standing Guatemalan refugee problems moved towards a successful conclusion thanks to a combination of voluntary repatriation and local integration in Mexico.

216. In other situations, however, continuing violence or a breakdown in political negotiations disrupted plans for refugees to return, leading in extreme cases to further exoduses. This was notably the case in Angola, where renewed hostilities caused a new wave of refugees and generated even greater numbers of internally displaced persons, forcing UNHCR to suspend its repatriation programme. Armed conflict in southern Sudan ruled out plans for the voluntary repatriation of some 240,000 refugees from Ethiopia and Uganda; some 124,000 Somali refugees in Kenya were likewise unable to return to their country of origin; around 120,000 Sahrawi refugees continued to live in exile, waiting for a successful conclusion to negotiations on Western Sahara; refugees from Burundi, numbering some 270,000, had to remain in the United Republic of Tanzania, where their presence was a major source of tension between the two States.

217. Solutions proved equally elusive in other parts of the world. In May 1998, internal conflict again broke out in Georgia, prompting 40,000 people to flee from the Gali area. Many were being displaced for the second time. The repatriation of Afghan refugees from Pakistan and the Islamic Republic of Iran was impeded by continuing instability in Afghanistan, where the reintegration and rehabilitation activities of UNHCR came to a virtual halt. The repatriation of hundreds of thousands of Tamil refugees to Sri Lanka from India proved impossible as a result of the intensity of the Sri Lankan civil war. UNHCR urged the Governments of Bangladesh and Myanmar to accelerate the voluntary repatriation of the estimated 20,000 Muslim refugees who remain in Cox's Bazar, Bangladesh. The repatriation programme resumed in November 1998.

218. The challenges facing UNHCR in these volatile and often stalemated situations are compounded by the fact that safe refuge in neighbouring States, or in countries further afield, is becoming increasingly difficult to secure for victims of war or human rights abuses. Countries in both the developing and the industrialized world are increasingly reluctant to accept the basic obligations of refugee protection. Poor countries argue that they have had to bear a disproportionate burden of the global refugee problem for too long.

219. Responding to these and other concerns, UNHCR has intensified its efforts under its protection mandate, giving prominence to advocacy activities such as the global campaign to promote States' accession to international instruments for the protection of refugees and to the conventions on statelessness. At the same time, it has taken steps to ensure that protection needs are better integrated into assistance programmes.

4 Engaging with globalization

220. Globalization is a summary term for the increasingly complex interactions between individuals, enterprises, institutions and markets across national borders. The manifold challenges it poses, challenges that cannot successfully be addressed by nation States acting on their own, provide the most immediate and obvious reason for strengthening multilateral cooperation. Globalization is manifest in the growth in trade, technology and financial flows; in the continuing growth and increasing influence of international civil society actors; in the global operations of transnational corporations; in the vast increase in transboundary communication and information exchanges, most notably via the Internet; in transboundary transmission of disease and ecological impact; and in the increased internationalization of certain types of criminal activity. Its benefits and risks are distributed unequally, and the growth and prosperity it provides for many are offset by the increasing vulnerability and marginalization of others—and by the growth of "uncivil society". During the past year, the United Nations has been examining the various dimensions of globalization—economic, social, environmental and gender—in some detail.

Economic and social dimensions

221. Only a year ago, a worldwide global recession was seen as a distinct possibility. Fortunately, such an outcome has thus far been avoided. Two years of crisis-induced international financial turbulence have nonetheless reduced global economic growth substantially. Other than Japan, the developed economies—conventionally viewed as the engines of growth in the world economy—have barely been affected, but the vast majority of developing and transition economies have experienced at the very least a slowdown—and in some cases a reversal—in economic growth, with its concomitant setbacks in social progress. The more favourable trends of the pre-crisis era may well be restored, but this will take time, and the losses of 1998 and 1999 can never be made up. Meanwhile, the world remains vulnerable to similar disruptions in the future, underlining the need for action to prevent such a possibility.

222. In the majority of countries, growth for the foreseeable future will fall short of what is necessary to reduce the number of people living in poverty. In developing countries as a whole, 1.5 billion people continue to live on less than $1 per day. Unfortunately, the commitment of the international community to the eradication of poverty has yet to produce results.

223. During the year, the United Nations provided a valuable platform for dialogue on the financial crisis, the persistence of poverty, the marginalization of Africa and the least developed countries and other dimensions of globalization.

224. At the intergovernmental level, the General Assembly is increasingly engaged with globalization issues. In September 1998, the Assembly held a two-day high-level dialogue on the theme of the social and economic impact of globalization. This innovative process, which involved ministerial round tables and panels, drew together perspectives from Governments, civil society, the private sector and the United Nations system and demonstrated the unique ability of the United Nations to engage a broad range of stakeholders on issues of critical importance to the international community.

225. Recognizing both the challenges and opportunities that today's globalized financial markets present, particularly for developing and transition economies, the General Assembly decided in 1997 to consider convening a high-level international intergovernmental forum on financing for development, not later than 2001. In the first half of 1999, the Working Group of the General Assembly on Financing for Development agreed that the forum would address national, international and systemic issues relating to financing for development in a holistic manner in the context of globalization and interdependence. The Working Group proposed that the forum involve all relevant stakeholders, including IMF and the World Bank. In this regard, the Economic and Social Council has recommended setting up a joint task force of United Nations and Bretton Woods institutions to facilitate the further involvement of those institutions in the finance for development process launched by the General Assembly.

226. The Economic and Social Council conducted a number of internal debates on the socio-economic dimensions of globalization during the year, and is working more and more with its counterparts in the Bretton Woods institutions in tackling these broad issues. The second special high-level meeting of the Economic and Social Council with the Bretton Woods institutions was held in 1999 and was complemented by a number of exchanges between the Council and the Executive Directors of the World Bank and IMF. A further visit to the Council in the autumn of 1999 by the Executive Directors of the Bank and IMF, following their annual meetings, is being arranged. The Development Committee recommended that the United Nations

further refine the principles and good practice in social policy prepared by the World Bank as follow-up to the World Summit for Social Development.

227. The functional commissions of the Economic and Social Council—those addressing social development, the advancement of women and population and development—continued their work on the follow-up to United Nations conferences. Each of these broad issues is profoundly affected by globalization. Major achievements were the finalization of the optional protocol to the Convention on the Elimination of All Forms of Discrimination against Women and the five-year review of the International Conference on Population and Development, conducted at a special session of the General Assembly in June/July 1999. At its substantive session of 1999 the Economic and Social Council focused on the related issues of poverty, employment and gender equality, and the development of Africa.

228. The impact of globalization on gender in the world of work is both important and complex. It is the focus of a major study, the *1999 World Survey on the Role of Women in Development*, which has involved ILO, UNCTAD, the Department of Economic and Social Affairs and the World Bank, and which I will submit to the General Assembly.

229. The Commission for Social Development considered the impact of globalization on access to social services and recommended greater international coordination in the planning and financing of such services. The Commission on Population and Development considered the relationship between population growth, structure and distribution and sustained economic growth and sustainable development. The deliberations of that Commission highlighted how demographic challenges are affected by globalization, particularly with respect to the international movement of people and the spread of infectious diseases such as HIV.

230. The Commission on Sustainable Development dealt with a number of important challenges posed by globalization, including the management of the oceans, tourism, which is one of the fastest growing industries in the world economy, and the development challenges confronting small island developing States. It has proposed, among other ideas, steps for strengthening the work of the General Assembly on ocean affairs and policy guidelines for sustainable tourism. It also looked at the Barbados Programme of Action for the Sustainable Development of Small Island Developing States for the review which is to take place in the General Assembly in September 1999.

231. The Commission on Human Rights, recognizing that the driving forces of globalization can have major implications for human rights, particularly in developing countries, requested all treaty bodies, special rapporteurs, independent experts and working groups to address the impact of globalization on human rights within their respective mandates. The Subcommission on the Promotion and Protection of Human Rights was asked to submit a comprehensive study on this issue to the Commission at its next session.

232. At Headquarters, the new management arrangements and other reforms have enabled the Secretariat and other bodies to contribute more effectively to the ongoing dialogue on globalization. The Deputy Secretary-General leads a task force of senior officials which is coordinating the United Nations response to a range of globalization issues. The Executive Committee on Economic and Social Affairs has issued reports on the need for the reform of the global financial architecture and on the debt problems of developing countries. New reports are being prepared on development finance and the social dimensions of macro-economic policy as a contribution to the debate on socio-economic questions related to globalization.

233. One of the consequences of globalization has been the reaffirmation of regional identity. Addressing regional issues and enhancing cooperation with regional institutions via the regional commissions remains central to the work of the Organization. During the past year, the regional commissions have provided the vehicle for in-depth consultations involving Governments and civil society on the agenda of the Millennium Assembly. Globalization has also become a major research focus for the regionally dispersed campuses of the United Nations University and many of the other United Nations research institutes around the world.

234. The challenges of globalization are too great for Governments and international organizations to deal with on their own. Meeting in October 1998, the Administrative Committee on Coordination placed the challenges arising from globalization and the adverse effects of the financial crisis centrally on its agenda. Following that meeting, the United Nations Development Group was requested to develop an action plan for United Nations country teams to work together with national partners in response to the challenges of globalization and the financial crisis in East Asia. Drawing on existing strategies, the plan presented a range of specific options under four broad areas of activity: (1) monitoring the impact of the crisis, particularly on vulnerable groups; (2) assisting individual countries to carry out the necessary structural and institutional reforms; (3) helping to strengthen and build basic social services and safety nets for the least fortunate; and (4) forging closer links with the World Bank.

235. At the first regular session of 1999 of the Administrative Committee on Coordination, in April, the members concluded that, to meet the challenges of globalization, the United Nations system needed to cooperate more effectively with the private sector and civil society, as well as with Governments. Cooperation can be deepened through partnerships, and it was for this reason that I proposed at Davos that the power and reach of the corporate sector be engaged to further the goals of the Organization. At the second regular session, in October 1999, the members of the Committee will endeavour to reach some overall conclusions on the capacity of the United Nations system to respond flexibly and effectively to the challenges of globalization in the next century.

236. Despite the need to involve all stakeholders in devising responses to globalization, much of the responsibility for addressing its negative consequences rests with the world's most advanced economies. That is why I wrote to the leaders of the G-8 prior to their summit in Cologne in June 1999, urging them to act to prevent the majority of the world's population being left on the margins of the global economy. I urged them to boost their own economic growth, to provide additional official development assistance and debt relief and to bring the representatives of the developing countries and economies in transition into the deliberations on a new international financial system. Although some progress has been made in these areas, far more needs to be done.

237. Progress was made at the Cologne summit on the issue of relieving the debt burden of the heavily indebted poor countries. However, financial and operational details still need to be discussed by the Ministers of Finance at the next session of the Interim Committee, and in the Economic and Social Council this year emphasis was placed on ensuring adequate financing for the full implementation of the G-7 decisions at Cologne. With regard to official development assistance the picture is bleak, however. Between 1990 and 1998, the share of GDP devoted to official development assistance in the developed economies fell from 0.33 per cent to 0.23 per cent.

238. Countries enter the global trading system from very different starting points, and globalization and liberalization affect them unevenly. There have been notable developing country successes where domestic reforms have provided increased dynamism to international trade and investment. Yet problems of access to markets, capital and technology remain pervasive, and many developing countries find it extremely difficult to make the institutional transformations necessary for a beneficial integration into the world economy. In November 1999, the third session of the Ministerial Conference of the World Trade Organization will be held at Seattle, and it now seems likely that the Conference will launch a new round of multilateral trade negotiations. In the Economic and Social Council this year, the idea of making this round into a "development round" enjoyed considerable support. A new trade and development round could provide major opportunities for developing countries to negotiate their integration into the world economic system on the basis of a positive agenda. UNDP and UNCTAD are joining forces to help developing countries to formulate negotiating positions for the Conference.

Globalization and the environment

239. Changes in the global environment do not respect national boundaries and represent one of the most critical challenges of globalization. Nowhere is this more evident than in the threats posed to the world's population by global warming. These threats can only be addressed by far-reaching multilateral agreement, but the political consensus necessary to achieve this has not been easy to obtain. The fourth session of the Conference of the Parties to the United Nations Framework Convention on Climate Change was held in Buenos Aires in November 1998 to begin the process of deciding the rules for implementation of the mechanisms agreed in Kyoto in 1997 and to adopt a two-year plan of action.

240. The Tenth Meeting of the Parties to the Montreal Protocol on Substances that Deplete the Ozone Layer was held at Cairo in November 1998. Its agenda focused on strengthening international efforts to reverse the destruction of the Earth's protective ozone layer. For the first time, it took up the challenge of making policies to protect the ozone layer consistent with the ongoing efforts to reduce emissions of the greenhouse gases that cause climate change.

241. In February 1999, at Cartagena, the Conference of the Parties to the Convention on Biological Diversity examined the risks that biotechnology may pose for biological diversity and human health, its socio-economic implications for developing countries and the relevance of biosafety concerns in developing a precautionary approach to risk prevention. The international community is pursuing a protocol on biosafety that, among other aims, seeks to ensure that living modified organisms are transported into countries only with their prior informed consent.

242. Headway continues to be made in the global chemical safety agenda. International consensus was finally reached on the need for a legally binding treaty to

promote chemical safety by preventing unwanted trade in hazardous chemicals and pesticides. In this regard, the Rotterdam Convention on the Prior Informed Consent Procedure for Certain Hazardous Chemicals and Pesticides in International Trade was opened for signature in September 1998. In January 1999, at the second negotiating session, solid progress was made in the drafting of a global treaty to reduce and eliminate environmental emissions and discharges of persistent organic pollutants. The Criteria Expert Group has now met. The third negotiating session will be held at Geneva in September 1999, and a series of regional workshops are planned.

243. The Global International Water Assessment, a major initiative led by UNEP and financed by the Global Environment Fund, was launched to assess key issues and problems facing the aquatic environment over the next four years. The Assessment focuses on the problems of shared, transboundary waters. It is designed not only to analyse current problems but also to develop scenarios for the future condition of the world's water resources. Policy options will be analysed with a view to providing sound scientific advice for decision makers and managers concerned with water resources.

244. At the European regional level, the third Ministerial Conference on Environment and Health was held in London in June 1999. The Protocol on Water and Health, attached to the United Nations/Economic Commission for Europe Convention on the Protection and Use of Transboundary Watercourses and International Lakes, was signed by 35 countries, including 16 countries in transition. The Conference built on foundations laid at previous environment and health conferences (Frankfurt, 1989, and Helsinki, 1994). It marked a new commitment to improving the environment and health in the twenty-first century in view of the need for international cooperation to deal with transboundary problems, such as air pollution, the continuing lack of access to safe water and sanitation, and transport, where solutions have yet to be found to the adverse effects of increasing traffic levels on health and the environment.

245. Achieving effective, legally binding agreements to safeguard the environment remains a major challenge, particularly with respect to creating environmentally sensitive international trade regimes. UNEP, together with UNCTAD, is analysing the social and environmental impact of the economic trends associated with globalization. It is focusing in particular on clarifying potential areas of conflict and convergence between the global trade and environmental agendas. It is also assessing the value of using economic instruments to help to implement environmental agreements.

246. UNEP has pursued my call at the World Economic Forum at Davos for engagement with the private sector, for example through the adoption of the International Declaration on Cleaner Production. There has also been substantial progress in the work of UNEP with the financial services industry and the telecommunication and tourism sectors, including through a new initiative with tour operators.

"Uncivil society"

247. Globalization has brought many benefits but it has also been associated with the unrelenting growth of cross-border illegal activities, which have created a netherworld economy, running into the hundreds of billions of dollars, which threatens the institutions of the State and civil society in many countries. Production, trafficking and abuse of illicit drugs and the spread of transnational organized crime are the main challenges faced by the Office for Drug Control and Crime Prevention, which consists of the United Nations International Drug Control Programme and the Centre for International Crime Prevention, in confronting "uncivil society".

248. At the twentieth special session of the General Assembly, Member States made a historic commitment to eliminate, or significantly reduce, the illicit cultivation of the opium poppy, coca bush and cannabis by 2008. The critical importance of demand reduction in the campaign to curtail drug consumption within 10 years was also highlighted.

249. On the supply side, the United Nations International Drug Control Programme is playing a catalytic role in developing an overall strategy for eliminating illicit crops and drug trafficking. This strategy is predicated on the assumption that the drug problem needs to be addressed holistically, which in turn requires close cooperation between the Programme and its national and international partners, as well as the international financial institutions. Reducing incentives to cultivate illegal crops requires improving the overall quality of life in rural communities; this in turn means that greater attention must be paid to providing farmers with legal economic alternatives, including basic health, education and social services. On the demand side, the Programme has launched a new initiative to assist Governments in establishing an epidemiological database that will inform officials about the extent and type of drug abuse occurring within their borders. This will help them to develop more effective prevention, treatment and rehabilitation policies.

250. The Centre for International Crime Prevention has continued to promote efforts to address the growing challenges of transnational crime. In March 1999, it launched three global programmes against transnational organized crime, trafficking in human beings and corruption. The Ad Hoc Committee on the Elaboration of a Convention against Transnational Organized Crime has made considerable headway in drafting the convention and its three protocols on trafficking in human beings, migrants and firearms.

251. The rapid expansion of the global financial system and the Internet has increased the challenges posed by money-laundering. In response, the global programme against money-laundering of the Office for Drug Control and Crime Prevention is currently designing a global initiative, the United Nations Offshore Forum, to be launched early in 2000, to prevent the misuse of the offshore financial sector for the laundering of criminal proceeds. The wider objectives of this initiative are to improve transparency in international transactions and to stimulate greater international cooperation in dealing with transnational criminal activity involving offshore financial centres. The global programme against money-laundering will also continue to help Governments to meet the commitment they made at the twentieth special session of the General Assembly to adopt national money-laundering legislation and programmes by 2003.

Implications of globalization for security

252. Globalization has a number of implications for global and national security, some positive, some negative. Global market forces can generate wealth and spread prosperity, but where development is uneven the result can be increased political tensions and risks of instability—as we have recently witnessed following the East Asian financial crisis. Ironically, the same crisis reduced defence spending in the region, checking what some had characterized as a regional arms race. In Western Europe, the logic of market forces has deepened European integration, giving all parties a clear vested interest in the peaceful resolution of inter-State disputes.

253. Many commentators see an important association between the spread of economic liberalism, which is one of the hallmarks of globalization, and the expansion of political liberalism. More than 60 per cent of the world's States now have some form of democratic government. Proponents of what has been called the "democratic peace thesis" point out that democracies almost never fight each other and have far lower levels of internal armed conflict than non-democracies. They argue that insofar as the expansion of market forces facilitates the emergence of democracy, globalization has a positive impact on global security.

254. Globalization also has a dark side. Global demand for particular commodities, such as timber, diamonds and drugs, has provided the funds that have allowed warring factions to sustain fighting over many years. The same Internet that has facilitated the spread of human rights and good governance norms has also been a conduit for propagating intolerance and has diffused information necessary for building weapons of terror.

255. Rising levels of industrial development also mean that more and more States have access to the basic technologies needed to make weapons of mass destruction, while the increasingly open global market makes controlling traffic in the precursors of weapons of mass destruction increasingly difficult.

5   The international legal order and human rights

Introduction

256. As the nineteenth century gave way to the twentieth, Peace Conferences held at The Hague in 1899 and 1907 sought to humanize our world and to introduce rules to mitigate human suffering during armed conflict. The quest for the peaceful settlement of disputes had as its *raison d'être* the reduction of human suffering wrought by war. The efforts of the League of Nations and the United Nations to codify and progressively develop international law have seen their greatest vindication in the twentieth century in the international legal regime for the protection of human rights.

257. Today, declarations, conventions, treaties, bodies of principles and codes of conduct cover almost every conceivable aspect of the relationship between the individual and the State. Legal instruments exist to protect the rights of the child, to protect the rights of women to equality of treatment, to spell out the duties of Governments in respect of the observance of civil and political rights and economic, social and cultural rights, to proscribe racial discrimination, to prevent torture, to protect minorities and to promote and protect cultural diversity. We enter the new millennium with an international code of human rights that is one of the great accomplishments of the twentieth century.

258. Alas, human rights are flouted wantonly across the globe. Genocide, mass killings, arbitrary and summary executions, torture, disappearances, enslavement, discrimination, widespread debilitating poverty and the persecution of minorities still have to be stamped out. Institutions and mechanisms have been established at the United Nations to eradicate these blights on our civilization. They include the working groups and special rapporteurs of the Commission on Human Rights, the institutions and mechanisms established to promote the realization of economic, social and cultural rights and the right to development, and the Office of the United Nations High Commissioner for Human Rights.

259. When we face egregious violations of human rights, documenting and exposing them has been, and will remain, of the utmost importance. In the future, it is our hope that the International Criminal Court, building on the examples set by the International Tribunals already established, will not only bring criminal despots and tyrants to justice but also act as a deterrent against gross violations of human rights everywhere.

260. The agreement reached to establish the International Criminal Court is a watershed in the history of international cooperation for the promotion of human welfare and for the universal realization of human rights. Developments in this area are of such great potential import for the international legal order that they warrant detailed attention.

The International Criminal Court

261. Eighty-four States have now signed the Rome Statute of the International Criminal Court. Four have ratified the statute, which will enter into force after ratification by 60 States. At the request of the General Assembly in December 1998, I convened the Preparatory Commission for

the International Criminal Court established by the Rome Conference. The Commission held its first session in February 1999 and its second in July-August. A third session will be held in November-December.

262. The Preparatory Commission has made some progress in drafting the Rules of Procedure and Evidence and the Elements of Crimes for the future Court, but much remains to be done if the deadline of 30 June 2000 set by the Rome Conference is to be met. In the meantime, I urge Member States to ratify the statute and take the necessary steps for its implementation.

The International Tribunals

263. At the request of the General Assembly in December 1998, I appointed five independent experts to review all aspects of the functioning of the two International Tribunals. The review is general in scope but will focus on judicial management, especially case management in the pre-trial phase. Its aim will be to ascertain whether resources can be deployed more efficiently. The review team is to report to the General Assembly towards the end of 1999.

264. The judgements of the two Tribunals have continued to clarify key aspects of international humanitarian law. These include the scope of grave breaches of the Geneva Conventions of 1949; the application of, and the distinction between, the concepts of international and non-international armed conflict; the rules of international humanitarian law which are applicable in armed conflict of a non-international character; the meaning and scope of crimes against humanity, including their relation to armed conflict; the definition of torture in international humani-

tarian law; the definition of rape in international criminal law; the criminality of the planning and preparation of violations of international humanitarian law; the meaning and scope of command responsibility; the legitimacy of duress as a defence against charges of war crimes and crimes against humanity; and elements of the offence of aiding and abetting in the planning, preparation or execution of a crime under international law.

265. Two main challenges confront the Tribunals. First, further steps must be taken to reduce the time the accused are held in custody awaiting trial and the time taken to conduct the trials themselves. Second, the Tribunal for the Former Yugoslavia faces the additional, and immense, task of investigating crimes committed in Kosovo.

International Tribunal for the Former Yugoslavia

266. In the past year, the International Tribunal for the Former Yugoslavia issued four indictments against nine individuals including, most notably, Slobodan Milosevic, President of the Federal Republic of Yugoslavia. Since its inception, the Tribunal has issued 27 public indictments against 90 individuals.

267. At the time this report was being prepared, the Tribunal was holding 30 people in custody. Five of those were awaiting appeals; 10 were being tried; 15 were awaiting trial. During the past year, the trials of eight accused were commenced, while judgements were handed down in respect of six accused, bringing the total of those subjected to judgement to seven. Five of the accused were found guilty of at least some of the charges against them; the other was found not guilty on all counts. In addition, the appeal of one accused against conviction and sentence

was rejected by the Appeals Chamber, which at the same time allowed appeals by the Prosecutor against his acquittal on certain counts.

268. During the year, the President of the Tribunal wrote four times to the President of the Security Council protesting at the failure of the Federal Republic of Yugoslavia to cooperate with the Tribunal, its continuing failure to arrest and transfer three persons indicted by the Tribunal and its persistent refusal to permit the Prosecutor and her investigators to enter Kosovo.

269. As a consequence of events in Kosovo, the Office of the Prosecutor established temporary operational bases in Albania and the former Yugoslav Republic of Macedonia. The Prosecutor also received my authorization to recruit up to 300 type-II gratis personnel from Member States to undertake specialized forensic work in Kosovo as soon as international forces were deployed. To date, 11 States have finalized agreements with the Organization to provide experts for this purpose.

270. Austria and Sweden concluded agreements on enforcing the sentences of the Tribunal, bringing to five the number of those agreements concluded to date. Negotiations are under way with other States to secure similar agreements.

271. On 16 October 1998, the General Assembly elected three judges to staff a new, third Trial Chamber. They took up their duties on 16 November 1998. Judge Gabrielle Kirk McDonald announced her resignation from the Tribunal, with effect from 17 November 1999. Following consultations with the Presidents of the Security Council and the General Assembly, I appointed Patricia McGowan Wald, a national of the United States of America, to serve out the remainder of Judge McDonald's term of office, which ends in November 2001. The Prosecutor of

the two Tribunals, Louise Arbour, announced her resignation with effect from 15 September 1999. On 11 August 1999, the Security Council appointed my nominee, Carla Del Ponte, a national of Switzerland, as Prosecutor of both Tribunals, effective 15 September 1999.

International Tribunal for Rwanda

272. During the past year, the International Tribunal for Rwanda issued two indictments against five individuals. Since its inception, it has served 28 indictments on 48 people. Thirty-eight people are currently in custody under the authority of the Tribunal; 5 accused are waiting for appeals to be heard; 3 are being tried; and 30 are awaiting trial. Five accused have already been found, or pleaded, guilty on counts involving genocide. All five have been sentenced. Appeals are pending from all of these judgements or sentences.

273. Mali became the first State to conclude an agreement on enforcing the sentences of the Tribunal. Negotiations are under way with other States for the conclusion of further such agreements.

274. On 3 November 1998, the General Assembly elected nine judges to the Tribunal's Trial Chambers. At the Tribunal's plenary session in June 1999, Judge Navanethem Pillay was elected President of the Tribunal, replacing Judge Laïty Kama, who was ineligible for re-election to that post.

The way forward

275. Throughout this report, I have sought to emphasize that peace, development and human rights are

interrelated. I have also noted that the combination of underdevelopment, globalization and rapid change poses particular challenges to the international human rights regime. This makes it doubly important that we insist on the responsibility of Governments to uphold human rights regardless of their political, economic, social or cultural systems and notwithstanding their economic and social situation. Stated simply: the pursuit of development, the engagement with globalization, and the management of change must all yield to human rights imperatives rather than the reverse.

276. Respect for human rights, as proclaimed in the international instruments, is central to our mandate. If we lose sight of this fundamental truth, all else will fail.

6 Managing change

Creating a culture of communication

277. The creation of a new culture of communication within the United Nations is central to our preparations for meeting the challenges of the twenty-first century. In pursuing this goal, the Department of Public Information is implementing a new outreach strategy, in partnership with organizations in civil society throughout the world. The aim is to find new ways to publicize United Nations activities and to highlight our successes. In support of this aim, the Department has worked during the year to promote greater openness and transparency by making more information more widely available, and by improving contact between United Nations officials and the world's media. At the same time, the United Nations programme for broadcasters and journalists from developing countries, which the Department sponsors and runs each year, is engaging younger generations of practitioners and helping to build networks of media professionals who can raise awareness of the work of the United Nations around the world.

278. The Department plans to improve the speed of delivery of United Nations news by initiating a Web-based United Nations News Service which will use e-mail to alert journalists to important news stories emanating from the Organization. Wherever possible, such news alerts will be tailored to the journalists' interests and will be linked to a United Nations News Centre on the home page which will provide greater details about each story outlined in the news alert. Tele- and videoconferencing press briefings by

senior United Nations officials from Headquarters and other news-making sites will also help to bring United Nations news to the desks of reporters around the world. United Nations information centres will play a key role by gathering supplementary information from regional centres and monitoring domestic media coverage.

279. The Department has overall responsibility for the United Nations Internet Web site, which is undergoing constant refinement. In 1999, a new audio-visual home page was created on the site. United Nations radio and television programmes are now available almost immediately to Internet users around the globe. The United Nations home page (www.un.org) is accessed 3 million times a week, from 133 countries. Use has increased dramatically over the past three years: from 11.5 million hits in 1996 to 98.5 million in 1998, and a projected 150 million in 1999. Intergovernmental support will be vital to sustain the Web site in all United Nations languages and keep it up to date, both in content and in the light of technological advances.

280. More than 800,000 schools from over 100 countries have accessed the Department's Cyberschoolbus (www.un.org/cyberschoolbus), an on-line interactive education project which brings together diverse communities of students and educators to learn about the work of the United Nations. The Schools Demining Schools project, for example, raised funds from schoolchildren in donor countries to help to clear mines around schools in war-torn countries. It also helped raise awareness about mines among students who corresponded by e-mail with mine-clearance teams in Afghanistan and Mozambique.

281. During the year, the Department presented a wide range of exhibitions and special events at Headquarters in New York and elsewhere in collaboration with United Nations agencies and outside partners, such as the

Walt Disney Company, the American Foundation for AIDS Research (AmFAR) and the Freedom Forum. The Department has received a record number of requests for assistance for projects to mark the year 2000.

282. Among its services to the general public, the Department continues to target young people through both direct, face-to-face contact—such as guided tours, briefings and special events—and workshops for students and teachers. In December 1998, almost 400 young people from 125 schools in seven countries attended a student conference on human rights at Headquarters. Videoconferencing is also an increasingly important means of connecting young audiences everywhere with the United Nations. In addition, a special effort is being made to involve young people from around the world in the global communications strategy for the Millennium Assembly.

283. To communicate effectively, the United Nations has to be able to get its message across to citizens of Member States as well as Governments. The United Nations information centres play a vital role here by organizing events and disseminating information in local languages that demonstrate how the work of the United Nations is relevant to the daily lives of people everywhere. Their presence on the ground and familiarity with local conditions allow the centres to deliver the Organization's message more effectively to domestic audiences. The United Nations global vision finds a local voice through the relationships that the centres develop with the local community.

284. During the past year, the information centres, in cooperation with Governments and non-governmental organizations, have focused on educational and youth activities, such as model United Nations conferences, after-school educational programmes and community service projects.

285. The Dag Hammarskjöld Library has further increased its "virtual library" capacity by using the Internet to link to United Nations depository libraries and other major libraries around the world. An increasing number of documents are now posted in Arabic, Chinese, French, Russian and Spanish, as well as English, while a new search engine guides users to major reference sources and the most frequently requested United Nations reports. A newsletter is distributed electronically to more than 330 depository libraries around the world, drawing their attention to newly released United Nations documents. The Library is offering on-line training courses and, as part of its outreach to civil society, particularly in developing countries, is conducting regional training programmes to draw attention to the availability of on-line information at the United Nations.

Administration and management

286. A new vision for management is central to my programme for the reform of the Organization. The strategy which is implementing that vision seeks to create simplified structures and a leaner and more efficient Secretariat run by empowered managers who are committed to managerial excellence and accountability. With the support of staff and management, we are making steady progress towards meeting our goals of streamlining procedures across a range of areas.

287. The Management Policy Office has established an ongoing dialogue with programme managers regarding the implementation of productivity measures that will improve the delivery of mandated programmes while containing, or reducing, costs. It is my intent that efficiency

savings will be deposited in a new Development Account and made available for additional projects.

288. Advanced information technologies have improved communication with staff and encouraged discussion on reform throughout the Organization. The Change Management Forum is the leading vehicle for debate, while the UN21 Awards have continued to recognize staff for innovative ideas. The establishment of a Human Resources Cyber Forum has allowed an on-line exchange of views on reform issues. The Ideas Data Bank, set up to encourage staff to offer ideas for management improvements, now contains almost 100 proposals.

289. We are committed to continue improving management practices, notably in reporting and monitoring systems and in enhancing management capacity and accountability.

Human resources management

290. The strategy for human resources management adopted by the General Assembly in 1994 was reconfirmed and expanded in 1996 and 1998. Implementation of the strategy is progressing steadily, with managerial delegation, empowerment and accountability being pursued on an incremental basis making use of a variety of monitoring mechanisms and the strengthening of specific methods of accountability.

291. An electronically accessible performance assessment system is now in place. It aligns performance appraisal more closely with results, identifies staff development needs and holds managers accountable for both managing and staff development. The streamlining of recruitment, placement and promotion procedures is under way and in its initial phase will halve the time needed for

each. A recently installed tracking capability will monitor progress.

292. We are building the managerial resources of the Secretariat through an integrated series of staff development and career support programmes. The introduction of a human resources review programme, which will culminate in action plans agreed with individual programme managers, has added a new dimension to human resources planning.

Financial management

293. The Department has continued to develop its results-based approach to financial budgeting. In line with this, current budget proposals include a parallel set of performance indicators, which will highlight the expected outcome for the resources committed. These will form the basis for a prototype budget to be submitted for review to the General Assembly by the autumn of 1999.

294. As in the past, we have provided Member States with regular updates on the financial situation of the Organization. This remains critical. Despite the fact that 117 Member States—a record high—met in full their regular budget assessments for 1998 and all prior years, as at mid-1999 the United Nations was still owed $2.5 billion. As a result, there has been no reduction in the debt to Member States for troops and equipment used in peacekeeping operations. This debt remains at almost $900 million—the same level as for the past three years. Unless there is a significant payment of arrears by Member States, we do not envisage paying off any of this debt in 1999. The United Nations therefore has little, if any, financial flexibility, and those Member States waiting for payment face few prospects for relief.

295. Concerns have recently grown over the added burden of some humanitarian and peacekeeping activities where the additional financing has not been forthcoming as promptly as required, or where the Organization has been asked to meet costs from funds already allocated for its regular programme of work.

Information technology

296. Upgrades to the Secretariat's information technology infrastructure have improved our ability to disseminate information internally and to Member States. Major achievements have included the replacement of more than 4,000 personal computers, the upgrading of the local area network, a rolling programme to install the latest industry-standard office automation software packages, and improvements to the satellite communication system, which can now support increased traffic from the main duty stations and peacekeeping missions. At the same time, the provision of electronic mail, greater technical support and the decision to host Web pages of permanent missions in New York have revolutionized communications with Member States.

297. We have continued our programme to develop and install an up-to-date integrated management information system (IMIS) at all duty stations. We are now testing the last elements of this system. At present, eight major duty stations use the system for personnel matters. All Headquarters financial management needs are also now met through the system; away from Headquarters, capability will be in place by the end of 2000. The new payroll capacity of the system will also be deployed by the end of 2000. Further technological advances will allow those working in the field to have remote access to the integrated management system. The system has become ever more versatile, and other United Nations agencies are installing it or those component features which are responsive to their needs.

298. We have made concerted efforts in the past year to ensure Y2K compliance. The Year 2000 Management Group identified core operations for the Organization as a whole and oversaw the drawing up of contingency plans in the event of breakdown of mission-critical operations. In addition, the Administrative Committee on Coordination reviewed the preparedness of members of the United Nations system and identified lead agencies to coordinate work in each location.

Facilities management

299. During the past year, we have given particular attention to the maintenance and renovation of the Headquarters complex of buildings, which has now been in constant use for almost 50 years. In response to growing overhaul and maintenance needs, we are drawing up a programme of long-term capital investment for the refurbishment of Headquarters. Coupled with our commitment to energy conservation programmes, this should help to improve the working environment for our staff and others who use our facilities.

Legal affairs

Legislative assistance

300. A number of bodies involved in the legislative process, in particular the International Law Commission and the United Nations Commission on International

Trade Law (UNCITRAL), benefited from the legal research services of the Office of Legal Affairs during the year. The Office also provided legal advice to law-making bodies to assist their deliberations and promote the successful conduct of their negotiations, including the International Law Commission; UNCITRAL; the Sixth Committee of the General Assembly and its working groups; the Ad Hoc Committee established by General Assembly resolution 51/210 of 17 December 1996; the Special Committee on the Charter of the United Nations and on the Strengthening of the Role of the Organization; the Preparatory Commission for the International Criminal Court; and the First Meeting of the States Parties to the Ottawa Convention.

301. The Office of Legal Affairs also provided assistance in running conferences convened for the negotiation and adoption of a number of important multilateral agreements and provided support to the institutions created by the United Nations Convention on the Law of the Sea (the Meeting of States Parties, the Commission on the Limits of the Continental Shelf, the International Seabed Authority and the International Tribunal for the Law of the Sea). Other international organizations sought advice from the Office in developing regulations, rules and standards in their respective areas of competence, for example, in the field of maritime law.

302. The Office participated in the drafting of several legal instruments, including my bulletin on fundamental principles and rules of international humanitarian law applicable to United Nations forces in situations of armed conflict.

303. The Office also provided guidance to States in taking measures for the implementation of the United Nations Convention on the Law of the Sea and offered technical assistance to States engaged in commercial law reform, targeting in particular those States considering the adoption of texts prepared by UNCITRAL.

Legal advice

304. The Office assisted in the preparation and drafting of agreements between the United Nations and a number of other international organizations. This assistance included helping to prepare a draft relationship agreement with the Preparatory Commission for the Comprehensive Nuclear-Test-Ban Treaty Organization. It also assisted in preparing and drafting agreements between the United Nations and individual States—most notably, status-of-mission agreements and agreements with States for the enforcement of the sentences of the two International Tribunals. The Office also provided legal assistance for the negotiation of contracts, leases and other legal transactions in which the Organization was involved.

305. Legal advice on a range of peacekeeping operations was provided, including the preparation of agreements between Indonesia and Portugal on the status of East Timor; between the United Nations and the International Organization for Migration and between the United Nations and Australia on the conduct of the popular consultation for East Timorese living outside East Timor; and on the status of the United Nations Mission in East Timor. It drafted appeals procedures and operational directives for the Identification Commission of the United Nations Mission for the Referendum in Western Sahara and prepared the legislative instruments necessary for the United Nations Interim Administration Mission in Kosovo (UNMIK) to commence operations and gave advice on a range of complex legal issues arising from that Mission's administration of Kosovo.

306. It followed up on the report of the Group of Experts for Cambodia and developed a proposal for a tribunal for the prosecution of Khmer Rouge leaders.

307. The Office of Legal Affairs also provided legal advice, assistance and representation in relation to the resolution of a number of disputes around the world. The Office represented the United Nations in suits brought by the Organization or against it, including a large number of commercial claims arising from peacekeeping missions. It acted to secure respect for the United Nations privileges and immunities by representing me before the International Court of Justice in the advisory proceedings concerning a *Difference Relating to Immunity from Legal Process of a Special Rapporteur of the Commission on Human Rights*. It also acted for the Organization before the two International Tribunals and drew up general guidance for the Secretariat on how to respond to requests from the Tribunals for access to United Nations documentation and for testimony from force commanders and other United Nations personnel.

308. The Office assisted the Member States concerned in the resolution of legal issues related to the implementation of Security Council resolution 1192 (1998), and other Council resolutions concerning the bombing of Pan Am flight 103. In addition, it was charged with the task of preparing for, and effecting, the transfer of the two persons suspected of the bombing from the Libyan Arab Jamahiriya to the Netherlands.

309. General guidance was provided to the Secretariat on the conduct of its business, and advice was given to political organs on questions of procedure, participation, representation and membership arising from their work. Legal advice was offered on questions relating to the enforcement of sanctions imposed by the Security Council and on implementing the oil-for-food programme.

310. The Office served as a focal point for contacts between the legal advisers of the United Nations system of organizations and promoted coordination between them on matters of legal policy.

International treaty system

311. The Office discharged my functions as depositary of 508 multilateral treaties. In the past year, the Office handled over 1,800 separate actions in connection with those treaties, considering and addressing the many legal questions arising. The Office discharged the Secretariat's function under the Charter of registering treaties and international agreements entered into by Member States, processing over 2,500 registration submissions during the past year.

Information outreach

312. A range of activities were undertaken during the year to improve the dissemination of information on international law and the work of United Nations legal bodies. In particular, the Office continued to implement a new programme aimed at promoting understanding of the United Nations Convention on the Law of the Sea and ensuring its consistent and effective application.

313. The Office made significant improvements to its publications programme. It reduced the backlog in the production of the *Treaty Series* and introduced measures that should eliminate it completely by 2001. It also increased efforts to address the backlog in the preparation of the *Repertory of Practice of United Nations Organs*. It set

up an electronic database for production of the monthly *Statement of Treaties and International Agreements Registered or Filed and Recorded with the Secretariat* and *Multilateral Treaties Deposited with the Secretary-General* and initiated measures to post all printed volumes of the *Treaty Series* on the Internet by 2001. It improved and updated its Web sites on the Organization's treaty collection, the International Law Commission, the International Criminal Court and the codification, development and promotion of international law.

314. The international law audio-visual library was expanded to facilitate loans of audio-visual material to Governments and educational institutions; and training seminars and briefing sessions on uniform commercial law were organized to promote awareness of texts prepared by UNCITRAL and encourage States to adopt them.

Challenges

315. In the year ahead, the Office anticipates major challenges in addressing the complex legal issues arising from the implementation of the mandate of UNMIK in Kosovo, and in assisting Member States in their preparations for the establishment of the International Criminal Court. Additional challenges are emerging from the upsurge of activity around the world aimed at reforming and modernizing commercial law and the concomitant need to harmonize and unify the laws of international trade.

Project services

316. The United Nations Office for Project Services, the only entirely self-financing entity in the United Nations system, executes projects on behalf of United Nations agencies and other organizations around the world. Among the many services it provides are project management, loan administration, procurement of goods and services and recruitment of project personnel. The Office combines corporate and public values, putting private sector practices at the service of the ideals of the Charter of the United Nations.

317. In 1998, the total project portfolio of the Office for Project Services reached $3.5 billion, and new business acquisitions exceeded $1 billion for the first time. Actual delivery amounted to $713 million. This represents the value of all inputs—goods, services and consultants—contracted by the Office to execute projects entrusted to it by its clientele. It also includes the authorization of $175 million in loan disbursements for projects that the Office is supervising for the International Fund for Agricultural Development.

318. The Office for Project Services continued to work on behalf of UNDP in such traditional areas as environmental management, governance and the eradication of poverty. It also worked with new partners, including the Department of Political Affairs, the Department of Peacekeeping Operations, the Office of the United Nations High Commissioner for Human Rights and the Office of the United Nations High Commissioner for Refugees, in areas outside the strict purview of development.

319. Several milestones in 1999 highlighted the benefits of new partnerships with other entities of the United Nations system. On behalf of the Department of Political Affairs, for example, support was provided to the Commission for Historical Clarification in investigating and documenting human rights abuses in Guatemala. The Office established the Commission's infrastructure, comprising 14 local offices in nine regions of the country, hired the interviewers who documented the country's long history of political violence, contracted services locally and internationally, procured equipment and provided training. The Commission presented its final report to me in February 1999.

320. The Office for Project Services also assisted the Electoral Assistance Division of the Department of Political Affairs, UNDP and the Government of Mexico in the production of a state-of-the-art CD-ROM, which provided guidelines on electoral assistance and was released in Mexico City in March 1999.

321. In June 1999, the Office's Mine Action Unit responded to the request of the Department of Peacekeeping Operations for assistance in laying the groundwork for United Nations mine-clearance operations in Kosovo—a prerequisite for the large-scale return of refugees. The Unit is setting up a Mine Action Coordination Centre in Pristina, hiring a manager and key personnel, and procuring equipment as needed. The Geneva Office, home of the Rehabilitation and Social Sustainability Unit, is well placed to provide management services to United Nations organizations engaged in the reconstruction of Kosovo.

322. The Office for Project Services has made client diversification a top priority so as to broaden its financial base and better serve the needs of the international community. In 1999, as part of its move towards decentralization, the Office signed an agreement with FAO and opened a regional office in FAO headquarters in Rome. The Office hopes that its presence there will encourage new alliances with other United Nations partners as well as bilateral and multilateral development organizations.

323. In keeping with its innovative approach, the Office for Project Services seeks where possible to turn challenges into opportunities. Its own work on Y2K compliance, for example, has translated into new projects in several countries to help Governments deal with the challenges posed by the "millennium bug". Relocation to new offices in autumn 1999 has led to the development of a new expertise in architectural and construction management that can be tapped by other members of the United Nations system. The Office now has teams for business and project development that can design services to match the changing needs of its many partners.

324. As the United Nations embarks on a new relationship with the private sector, it can benefit from the experience of the Office for Project Services in outsourcing from, and working with, business to adopt best corporate practice while remaining faithful to the principles of the Charter.

Accountability and oversight

325. In its fifth year of existence, the Office of Internal Oversight Services has continued to strive for increased management accountability within the Organization. During this period, a culture of internal oversight has become accepted and strengthened, and the working methods of the Office have become well established.

326. The Office of Internal Oversight Services has developed a number of mechanisms for enhancing internal oversight of separately administered organs. It has concluded memoranda of understanding for the provision of internal audit services with the Office of the United Nations High Commissioner for Refugees, the International Trade Centre UNCTAD/WTO and the United Nations Compensa-

tion Commission. Audit services are also provided to the United Nations International Drug Control Programme and the United Nations Joint Staff Pension Fund. These arrangements have operated for several years and reflect the commitment of the Office to promoting sound management and accountability throughout the United Nations system.

327. The Fifth Committee of the General Assembly and the Committee for Programme and Coordination have taken an increasing interest in the work of the Office of Internal Oversight Services. The number of reports published by the Office has increased each year, more than 50 per cent being in response to mandates from the General Assembly.

328. In 1999, the Office of Internal Oversight Services has looked in particular at peacekeeping operations, humanitarian and other field-related activities, as well as the progress achieved in the Secretariat and its overseas offices in preparing information technology systems for the year 2000. Special emphasis was given to monitoring the progress of implementing United Nations reform, particularly in human resources management and other support services.

Audit and management consulting

329. During the past year, the Audit and Management Consulting Division of the Office of Internal Oversight Services conducted audits of various Secretariat activities, including administrative support, peacekeeping missions and technical cooperation projects; the United Nations Offices at Geneva, Nairobi and Vienna; the Office of the Humanitarian Coordinator in Iraq; the field operation in

Rwanda of the Office of the United Nations High Commissioner for Human Rights; the United Nations International Drug Control Programme projects in China, Thailand and the Netherlands Antilles; the Centre for International Crime Prevention and its International Scientific and Professional Advisory Council; UNEP and its Regional Office for West Asia and Regional Coordination Unit for East Asian Seas; the Fukuoka and Rio de Janeiro offices of the United Nations Centre for Human Settlements (Habitat); the United Nations Compensation Commission; and the International Tribunals for the Former Yugoslavia and Rwanda. Audits were also conducted at the Economic and Social Commission for Western Asia, the secretariat of the Economic Commission for Latin America and the Caribbean and its subregional headquarters for the Caribbean, the Economic Commission for Africa and the Economic Commission for Europe.

330. Peacekeeping operations and other field activities continued to receive priority. The Audit and Management Consulting Division conducted audits of peacekeeping missions in Angola, Bosnia and Herzegovina, Eastern Slavonia, Haiti, Israel, Lebanon and the Syrian Arab Republic, and the United Nations Logistics Base at Brindisi, Italy. In addition, the Division has assigned resident auditors to the United Nations Mission in Bosnia and Herzegovina, the United Nations Observer Mission in Angola and the Office of the Humanitarian Coordinator in Iraq.

331. The UNHCR Section of the Division audited UNHCR field operations in 20 countries. These audits, which also covered implementing partners, including government agencies and local and international non-governmental organizations, have contributed to improved internal controls and financial reporting. The Section paid particular attention to procurement to ensure

that this was fair and transparent, even under emergency conditions.

332. Recognizing the need to make the United Nations computer system Y2K-compliant, the Audit and Management Consulting Division participated as an ex officio member of the Headquarters year 2000 implementation team. It also conducted a major campaign to raise awareness at offices outside Headquarters by sending year 2000 questionnaires and follow-up reports to 22 offices, programmes and regional commissions around the world. The Division also conducted information technology audits of the United Nations Office at Nairobi and the International Tribunals for the Former Yugoslavia and Rwanda, and undertook a special consultancy to assist the International Computing Centre at Geneva in assessing the adequacy, timeliness and completeness of its planning and preparations for meeting the year 2000 problem.

333. The Office of Internal Oversight Services submitted the results of several audits and reviews to the General Assembly at its fifty-third session, including those of the United Nations health insurance programme, the employment of retirees, the increase in costs of the development contract for the Integrated Management Information System, and the review of procurement-related arbitration cases.

Evaluation

334. The Office of Internal Oversight Services reviewed the support given by the Department for Disarmament Affairs to international disarmament bodies, namely, the First Committee of the General Assembly, the Disarmament Commission and the Conference on Disarmament.

The Office found that delegations were generally satisfied with the level of support provided by the Department to multilateral bodies. The evaluation did, however, identify a number of shortcomings related to the activities of the regional centres; the United Nations Disarmament Information Programme; technical information provided to Member States; cooperation with regional organizations; and development of contacts with specialized agencies, research bodies and non-governmental institutions.

335. The Office of Internal Oversight Services assessed the achievements of the United Nations electoral assistance programme from 1992 to 1998. The final report focused on (*a*) the role of the Electoral Assistance Division of the Department of Political Affairs in the context of the changing nature of the electoral assistance network, and international norms and codes of practice; (*b*) overlapping roles and responsibilities in the area of electoral assistance among units and organizations of the United Nations system; (*c*) internal and external assessments of the Electoral Assistance Division's major activities; and (*d*) the adequacy of existing standard operating procedures and lessons-learned processes.

336. The Office of Internal Oversight Services also conducted triennial reviews of the implementation of the recommendations made by the Committee for Programme and Coordination at its thirty-sixth session on the evaluation of the Department of Public Information and of the termination phase of peacekeeping operations. The review of the Department of Public Information found that the Department was acting on a number of the Committee's recommendations: it was using traditional media, such as radio, and new electronic media more actively, and it was developing a more effective news-gathering and delivery

system. However, progress was uneven and the effect of measures adopted in 1997 and 1998—following the reorientation of United Nations public information activities—will have to be reviewed again later.

337. The review of peacekeeping operations found that the Department of Peacekeeping Operations has made significant advances in learning lessons from past experience, in collaborating with the Department of Public Information on the information aspects of peacekeeping missions, and in closing down missions. However, there was little progress on establishing an indexed archive of standard operating procedures developed by completed missions. The Office will keep this issue under review.

Inspection and monitoring

338. In response to concerns raised by the Committee for Programme and Coordination at its thirty-eighth session on the need to place more emphasis on qualitative analysis in future programme assessments, the Office prepared a report on ways in which the full implementation and the quality of mandated programmes and activities could be ensured and could be better assessed by and reported to Member States. Three options were proposed, which were considered by the Committee at its thirty-ninth session. The Committee requested me further to explore ways in which the full implementation of mandates could be ensured and better assessed, in accordance with General Assembly resolution 53/207, and to report on this matter to the Committee at its fortieth session.

339. Progress in building up the provision of common services and improving the efficiency of support services in New York, Geneva and Vienna in the areas identified

in the programme for reform was also reviewed during the past year. The review revealed that the reform process had provided new impetus to improve cost-effectiveness through the expansion of common services. In its inspection report, the Office of Internal Oversight Services recommended measures to enhance central support services, and to remove barriers to the expansion of common services, such as distrust, "turf" protection and the lack of communication among heads of organizations. It also stressed the need for Member States to support fully the strengthening of common services.

Investigations

340. The Investigations Section of the Office of Internal Oversight Services, based in New York and Nairobi, continued to promote the principle of accountability by recommending that staff and contractors be held responsible for violations of United Nations rules and criminal acts perpetrated against the Organization. As provided by its mandate, the Section was involved in a range of inquiries. In 1999, the Section investigated allegations of corruption, examined partnerships with the private sector and completed its first investigation at a regional commission. The Section also worked with national law enforcement agencies to help bring before the courts those who had committed criminal acts against the Organization. One case involved the theft of $400,000 worth of United Nations property by a contractor to a peacekeeping mission. Another involved fraudulent travel expenses in a peacekeeping mission amounting to an estimated $1.2 million.

341. The Section investigated allegations of corruption in a major programme's field office. The investigation concluded that the evidence did not support the allegations. However, the Section recommended that the programme's management establish policies and procedures for investigating allegations impartially, expeditiously and transparently. This case represented a major step in the Organization's determination to enforce high ethical and legal standards in its commercial dealings with outside entities.

342. Following reports of the illegal export and improper retention of intellectual property by those associated with another programme's project, the Section examined United Nations/private sector partnerships involving electronic commerce. The investigation uncovered extensive solicitations of funds and unauthorized commercial agreements between United Nations staff and private individuals and companies. It also uncovered private sector interests in a United Nations–sponsored programme providing technical assistance to economically disadvantaged countries. The Office of Internal Oversight Services made recommendations to remedy these abuses and for tighter controls on private sector partnerships. The Senior Management Group has now formally taken up this question.

343. A review, conducted jointly with the Audit and Management Consulting Division, of the International Tribunal for the Former Yugoslavia disclosed that the three organs of the Tribunal—the Chambers, the Office of the Prosecutor, and the Registry—were generally managed in an efficient and effective manner. The review recommended improvements in some key administrative and financial areas, however. A report has been submitted to the General Assembly.

344. The Investigations Section also conducted proactive investigations throughout the Organization examin-

ing the potential for fraud and made recommendations to combat this. The investigations focused on staff entitlements, such as education and security grants, which are susceptible to abuse.

Index

*(The numbers following the entries refer to
paragraph numbers in the report.)*

A

Accountability, 50, 286, 289-290, 325-344

Administrative Committee on Coordination, 146, 174, 234-235, 298

Afghanistan, 6, 38, 83, 190, 199-200, 217, 280

Africa, 9, 58, 71-81, 97, 103, 143, 161, 166, 168, 172-187, 194, 200, 211, 214-215

Agenda 21, 170. *See also* Environment

AIDS, 143, 160, 164-166, 172, 181, 281

Angola, 2, 8, 89-90, 109, 190, 200-201, 216, 330

Arms limitation, 43-44, 118, 122, 199, 250

Arms trade. *See* Illicit arms transfers

Asia and the Pacific, 6, 119, 138, 141, 143, 147, 149, 151, 161, 166, 187, 211, 234, 252, 329

Aziz, Tariq, 81

B

Barbados Programme of Action for the Sustainable Development of Small Island Developing States, 230

Biodiversity Convention, 170, 241

Bretton Woods Institutions, 135, 141, 225-226

Burundi, 75, 200, 216

Business community, 137, 181, 324

C

Capacity-building, 141, 196

Central Africa, 72, 97, 103

Central Asia, 119, 141

Centre for International Crime Prevention, 247, 250, 329

Charter of the United Nations, 58, 66, 69, 300, 311, 316, 324

Children, 121, 149, 158-159, 182, 188-189, 200, 204-206, 280. *See also* United Nations Children's Fund

Cities Alliance, 150

Civil society, 25, 39-40, 53, 107, 136, 151, 161, 181, 205, 220, 224, 233, 235, 247, 277, 285. *See also* Governance; Nongovernmental organizations

Civilian police operations, 85

Climate, 35, 170, 189, 239-240. *See also* Environment

Commercial law, 303, 314-315

Commission on Human Rights, 231, 258, 307

Commission on Population and Development, 229

Commission on Sustainable Development, 167, 171, 230

Commodities, 20, 203, 254

Communications, 94, 282-283, 296

Comprehensive Nuclear-Test-Ban Treaty, 120, 304

Conference of the Parties to the United Nations Framework Convention on Climate Change, 239

Conference on Disarmament, 123, 334

Conflict prevention, 36, 39, 42, 47, 53, 58, 69

Conflict resolution, 56, 63

Convention on Certain Conventional Weapons, 121

Convention on the Elimination of All Forms of Discrimination against Women, 227

Convention on the Prior Informed Consent Procedure for Certain Hazardous Chemicals and Pesticides in International Trade, 242

G

Gender issues, 130, 134, 142, 147, 149, 153, 159, 185, 199-200, 206, 220, 227-228. *See also* Women

General Assembly, 160, 224-225, 271, 274

4th Special Session on Disarmament, 153, 227

Special Session to Review Implementation of the Fourth World Conference on Women, 152

20th Special Session on the World Drug Problem, 248, 251

21st Special Session on the International Conference on Population and Development, 152-153, 227

Genocide, 41, 258, 272

Girls, 135, 158, 189

Global Environment Facility, 170

Globalization, 135, 147, 177, 220-255, 275-276

Governance, 25, 45, 51-54, 109, 139, 150, 185, 209, 254, 318. *See also* Civil society

Great Lakes Region (Africa), 200. *See also* Burundi; Rwanda

Greenhouse gases, 240. *See also* Environment

Guatemala, 45, 103, 105, 215, 319

H

Haiti, 107, 330

Hazardous materials, 242

Health, 6, 142, 154, 158, 164-166, 188-189, 200, 203, 241, 244, 249

Human resources management, 288, 290-292, 328

Human rights, 45, 53, 62, 64-67, 76, 96, 104-108, 133, 139-140, 145, 154, 159, 199, 213, 218, 231, 254, 256-260, 275-276, 282, 319

Human settlements, 150, 156, 179

Humanitarian assistance, 96, 191, 198, 206

I

Illicit arms transfers, 44, 250, 255

India, 5-6, 217

Indonesia, 6, 85, 305

Information dissemination, 105, 132, 155, 177, 203, 207, 220, 277-278, 283, 285, 296, 312, 336-337

Inter-Agency Standing Committee, 195, 198-199, 206

International Conference on Population and Development, 152-153, 183, 227

International Court of Justice, 307

International Criminal Court, 65, 259-262, 300, 313, 315

International Criminal Tribunal for Rwanda, 272

International Criminal Tribunal for the Former Yugoslavia, 265-271, 343

International Decade for Natural Disaster Reduction, 28, 30, 35, 197

International Fund for Agricultural Development (IFAD), 146, 317

International humanitarian law, 100, 264, 302

International law, 66, 69, 193, 256, 264, 312-314

International Law Commission, 300, 313

International Monetary Fund (IMF), 138, 145, 225-226

International trade, 187, 238, 245

International trade law, 242, 315

International Tribunal for the Law of the Sea, 301

Internet, 27, 137, 220, 251, 254, 278-280, 285, 288, 296, 313

Iraq, 81, 125, 203, 330

J

Joint and Co-sponsored United Nations Programme on HIV/AIDS, 166. *See also* AIDS

Refugees, 64, 169, 209-219, 321. *See also* Displaced persons

Regional Commissions, 129, 148, 233, 332

Reproductive health, 153-154, 161, 183, 189. *See also* Health

Resident Coordinators, 130, 133, 146, 154

Rwanda, 41, 67, 200, 272-274, 329, 332

S

Sanctions, 62, 81, 124-126, 309

Secretariat, 100, 116, 141, 171, 232, 296, 307, 309, 311, 328-329

management, 286-292

oversight, 325-344

staff, 94-95, 201, 286, 288, 290-292, 299, 340, 342, 344

Secretary-General, 100, 188

Deputy, 174, 232

good offices, 37, 79, 105-106

reports, 3, 58, 145, 173, 193

Security Council, 58-59, 62, 66-69, 74, 76, 81-82, 85, 113, 124, 191, 193, 203, 205, 268, 271, 308-309

Sierra Leone, 190, 200, 214. *See also* United Nations Observer Mission in Sierra Leone

Social development, 152-166, 173, 227

Southern African Development Community, 73, 141

Southern African region, 178

Special Representative for Children and Armed Conflict, 205

Sudan, 79, 190, 200, 215-216

Sustainable Cities Programme, 179

Sustainable development, 22, 50, 58, 139, 167-171, 173, 178, 209, 229-230

Suu Kyi, Aung San, 86

T

Technical assistance, 121, 187, 303, 342

Telecommunications, 246

The former Yugoslav Republic of Macedonia, 42, 212, 269

Torture, 257-258, 264

Training programmes, 133, 285, 314

Twenty/Twenty (20/20) initiative, 162-163

U

UN system, 158, 168, 174, 224, 235, 298, 310, 316, 319, 323, 326, 335

UN Web site, 279, 313

UNAIDS. *See* Joint and Co-sponsored United Nations Programme on HIV/AIDS

United Nations, 1, 36, 44-45, 58, 113-116, 127

budget, 293-294

cooperation with other organizations, 76, 99, 116, 233

United Nations Centre for Human Settlements (Habitat), 150, 168, 179, 329

United Nations Children's Fund, 136-137, 148, 156, 158, 161-162, 166, 180-181, 200, 204, 206

United Nations Conference on Human Settlements (Habitat II), 150, 152

United Nations Conference on Trade and Development (UNCTAD), 150, 186-187, 228, 238, 245, 326

United Nations Convention on the Law of the Sea, 301, 303, 312

United Nations Development Assistance Frameworks, 129, 134

United Nations Development Fund for Women, 149, 155-156, 161, 166, 185

United Nations Development Group, 127, 130, 133, 135, 137, 140, 146-147, 158, 168, 172-173, 175, 234

United Nations Development Programme (UNDP), 106, 136-137, 139, 145, 148-150, 161-162, 166, 168-170, 177-179, 181, 186, 197, 209, 238, 318, 320

United Nations Drug Control Programme, 151, 160, 166, 181, 247, 249, 326, 329. *See also* Drug control

United Nations Educational, Scientific and Cultural Organization (UNESCO), 150, 161, 166, 180-181, 186

United Nations Environment Programme (UNEP), 168, 170, 179, 243, 245-246, 329

United Nations Framework Convention on Climate Change, 170, 239

United Nations Fund for International Partnerships, 188

United Nations High Commissioner for Human Rights, 76, 139, 195, 213, 258, 318, 329

United Nations High Commissioner for Refugees (UNHCR), 169, 200, 211-212, 215-219, 318, 326, 331

United Nations Houses, 132

United Nations Information Centres (UNICs), 278, 283-284

United Nations International Drug Control Programme, 151, 160, 166, 181, 247, 249, 326, 329

United Nations Mission in the Central African Republic (MINURCA), 97, 103

United Nations Observer Mission in Angola (MONUA), 90, 330

United Nations Observer Mission in Sierra Leone (UNOMSIL), 76, 91

United Nations Office for Drug Control and Crime Prevention, 247, 251

United Nations Office for Project Services, 316-324

United Nations Office in Nairobi, 329, 332, 340

United Nations Offshore Forum, 251

United Nations Political Office in Bougainville, 87

United Nations Population Fund (UNFPA), 136, 141, 148-149, 156, 161-162, 166, 181, 183

United Nations Preventive Deployment Force, 90

United Nations Relief and Works Agency for Palestine Refugees in the Near East, 210

United Nations Special Mission to Afghanistan, 83

United Nations University, 17, 47, 233

United Republic of Tanzania, 74, 180, 216

Urban Management Programme, 179

V

Vulnerability assessment mapping, 178

W

War crimes, 262, 264-265

Water resources, 243

Watercourses, 244

Western Sahara, 80, 216, 305

Women, 121, 142, 145, 149, 152-153, 155-156, 158, 166, 178, 182, 184, 188-189, 206, 227-228, 257

World Bank, 97, 138, 145, 148, 150, 162, 166, 168, 170, 179-181, 199, 225-226, 228, 234

World Conference on Human Settlements (Habitat II), 150, 152. *See also* Human settlements

World Conference on Women (4th), 152, 158. *See also* Women

World Food Programme (WFP), 136, 146, 149, 169, 178, 184, 200-202

World Health Organization (WHO), 166, 198, 203

World Meteorological Organization, 27

World Summit for Social Development, 152, 226. *See also* Social development

World Trade Organization (WTO), 186-187, 238, 326

Y

Youth, 159-161, 164, 277, 282, 284

United Nations publications
of related interest

*The following UN publications may be obtained from the addresses
indicated below, or at your local distributor:*

Basic Facts about the United Nations
E.98.I.20   92-1-100793-3   368pp. $10.00

Yearbook of the United Nations 1996, Vol. 50
E.99.I.1   90-411-1042-9   1552pp. $150.00

*UN Briefing Papers: Human Rights Today
A United Nations Priority*
E.98.I.22   92-1-100797-6   86pp. $12.00

Demographic Yearbook 1998, Vol. 50
B.00.XIII.1   92-1-051089-5 $150.00

Blue Helmets, The: A Review of United Nations Peace-keeping
E.96.I.14   92-1-100611-2   840pp. $29.95

*World Economic and Social Survey 1999:
Trends and Policies in the World Economy*
E.99.II.C.1   92-1-109135-7   270pp. $55.00

Statistical Yearbook, 43rd Edition
B.98.XVII.1   92-1-061180-2   922pp. $125.00

*World Concerns and the United Nations: Model Teaching Units
for Primary, Secondary and Teacher Education*
E.98.I.9   92-1-100651-1   192pp. $19.95

United Nations and Global Commerce, The
E.99.I.18   92-1-100815-8   78pp. $7.50

United Nations Publications
2 United Nations Plaza
Room DC2-853
New York, NY 10017
United States
Tel: (212) 963-8302, (800) 253-9646
Fax: (212) 963-3489

United Nations Publications
Sales Office and Bookshop
CH-1211 Geneva 10
Switzerland
Tel: 41 (22) 917-26-13, 917-26-14
Fax: 41 (22) 917-00-27

Report on the work of the Organization